Commitment to Place:
Urban Excellence & Community

Bruner Foundation, Inc.

Robert Shibley
with
Emily Axelrod, Jay Farbstein, and Richard Wener

1999 Rudy Bruner Award for Urban Excellence

Graphic Design:
Caronchi Industries
14 Sullivan Street
Charlestown, MA 02129
www.caronchi.com

Library of Congress Catalog Card Number: 99-76056
ISBN: **1-890286-03-6**

130 Prospect Street
Cambridge, MA 01239

Dedicated to

William H. Whyte, 1918-1999

(Rudy Bruner Award Selection Committe, 1987)

"I end, then, in praise of small spaces (in cities)...It is not just the number of people using them, but the larger number who pass by and enjoy them vicariously, or the even larger number who feel better about the city center for knowledge of them. For a city, such places are priceless, whatever the cost. They are built on a set of basics and they are right under our noses. If we look."

"Street Life," Conservation Foundation, New York, New York 1980, p.101

CONTENTS

PREFACE

It is a great pleasure for me to introduce to you the winners of the 1999 Rudy Bruner Award for Urban Excellence, and through them, to celebrate some innovative thinking about urban placemaking. As an architect, I have had the opportunity to do some thinking about cities, about urban architecture, and about what makes an excellent urban place. Urban architecture at its best is not about buildings that flash their way to the covers of magazines, but instead deals with architecture as a multidimensional whole and with the complex relationship between process, place, and values. It is rooted in good design that balances opportunity with cost; shape with use; and past with future. It incorporates a myriad of social, political, corporate, community, environmental, and formal issues into an inclusive and multi-dimensional architecture.

Because of my belief in the importance of this balance in architecture, I founded the Rudy Bruner Award for Urban Excellence, which is designed to recognize and celebrate innovative thinking about urban places, and to promote a dialogue about the nature of urban excellence. The Rudy Bruner Award is based on the belief that excellence in the built environment is about quality places that reflect the successful integration of three critical elements: thoughtful process, meaningful values, and good design. Our winners are urban places that are not only excellent in their own right, but relate in important ways to their urban contexts, and thus enrich the quality of urban life.

I have traveled the country over the past 12 years, visiting more than 35 Rudy Bruner Award winners and finalists. From these travels I can say unequivocally that this is a very exciting time in the history of American cities and urban architecture. For the first time in many years cities are included in – and in some cases are at the top of – our national agenda. Increasingly, resources are available to develop and revitalize some of our most neglected urban areas. And there are ideas out there! Yerba Buena Gardens represents the maturation of the urban redevelopment process. It has evolved into a rich mix of uses that serves a wide variety of constituencies with housing, cultural amenities, open space, and recreational and educational opportunities for San Francisco's youth. The National AIDS Memorial Grove is one of a very few memorials of its kind in the country, and is unique in its successful effort to restore a neglected corner of Golden Gate Park into a living memorial to the thousands who died of AIDS and to those whose lives have been deeply affected by this devastating epidemic. Through a grassroots effort AIDS victims have been publicly honored, and those who have lost loved ones have created a living monument to their memory.

In Los Angeles a coalition of community activists have turned abandoned lots in the inner city into "art parks," created and "owned" by neighborhood residents who have cleared the sites and created dynamic art statements that reflect community cultural values. In Philadelphia, historic housing in one of the city's poorest neighborhoods has been painstakingly restored by a neighborhood resident who has used a combination of financial tools to create affordable housing and office space for critical social services supporting the local community. In Portland, Maine a farsighted philanthropist invested in "economic philanthropy," creating a new public market in a marginal neighborhood adjacent to the downtown. The Market has brought a handsome new building to the neighborhood, brought many constituencies together, and is providing an important retail outlet for Maine farmers through a careful selection of vendors.

Several of the 1999 winners are young projects, still very much in process. But like many past RBA winners they are the products of visionary thinking, dedicated leaders, and a strong combination of effective processes, meaningful values, and good design. They have taken new or untried ideas and put them to work in their respective cities to create places that improve the quality of life in their neighborhoods. We encourage you to learn from what they have done, to use their ideas and adapt them to your own urban areas, and to think beyond what you have seen in creating exciting new urban places.

We at the Rudy Bruner Award hope that these exciting urban places will provide you with some food for thought, and with some potential solutions to the problems facing your own cities. These projects, and many other Award winners, teach us how to identify strengths in even the most troubled urban settings, and to build on those strengths to create excellent urban places. They are examples of what can be done, and perhaps more importantly, of what you can do. We encourage you to use these winners as resources for the hard work of creating excellent urban places. Good Luck!

Simeon Bruner, *Founder*

Simeon Bruner at San Francisco Award Presentation

INTRODUCTION: MAKING PLACES, BUILDING COMMITMENT

Since its inception in 1987, the Rudy Bruner Award for Urban Excellence has occupied a unique position among urban design awards. Typically, such awards have examined design in the narrow sense, recognizing the quality of imaginatively conceived or elegantly constructed places. The Rudy Bruner Award takes a different approach: "architectural" in the most comprehensive sense of the term, it is dedicated to discovering and celebrating places that are distinguished not only by their quality design, but by their social, economic, and contextual contributions to their urban environments. Looking beyond form, the Award asks how projects fit into and improve their urban context on many levels. While this does not negate the importance of good design, it does alter the boundaries of what good design means, placing new emphasis on the complex processes of collaboration required to create an excellent urban place.

In its 12-year history, the Rudy Bruner Award has recognized 37 winners from across the country that have exemplified its broader idea of urban excellence – places that arrived at good design through a thoughtful process powered by varied and deeply felt values. The criteria for entering the competition are intentionally broad, and the winners have been a diverse group that have made very different contributions to America's cities. Many represent new models of urban placemaking guided by creative visions that have successfully challenged conventional wisdom. Most are products of hard-won collaborations between very different people with very different agendas. All have lent vitality to the neighborhoods in which they are located. By celebrating their success, the Rudy Bruner Award highlights the complex process of urban placemaking, emphasizing the many elements beyond good design that produce urban excellence. Through studying the development and functioning of these projects, we can discover creative ways to respond to some of our cities' most intractable problems.

The Rudy Bruner Award also serves as a national forum on the nature of urban excellence. Rather than approaching projects with a set of preconceived standards, the Award seeks to flesh out its ideals through winners' own demonstrations of excellence. In essence, the Award hopes to find and understand, rather than to dictate, urban excellence. To ensure a lively process not dominated by any one perspective, each Selection Committee brings together a distinguished panel representing several different kinds of urban expertise, including architects, developers, community organizers, philanthropists, financiers, and the mayor of a major metropolitan area. As the Selection Committee discusses the project applications, they consider a wide variety of questions: What kinds of places make neighborhoods and cities better places to live, work, and play? How did these places come into being? What visions powered their creation? How did these visions become a reality? What obstacles had to be overcome? What makes a place important in its urban context? In this way the Selection Committee explores the dynamic nature of urban excellence and contributes to a broader understanding of the critical urban issues of the day.

ELIGIBILITY CRITERIA

The Award's eligibility criteria have been specifically designed to cast a wide net, so that even places not traditionally associated with "architectural" excellence can make their case. First, the project must be a real place, not a plan. It must exist and be able to demonstrate its excellence to a distinguished Selection Committee. And second, the project must be located in the United States. Site visits are integral to the award process, and it is not currently possible to conduct visits to international locations.

THE 1999 SELECTION COMMITTEE (in alphabetical order)

Curits M. Davis, AIA,
John Hancock Mutual Life Insurance Co., Boston
Lawrence Goldman,
President/CEO, New Jersey Performing Arts Center, Newark
Min Kantrowitz, AICP, MArch,
President, Min Kantrowitz and Assoc., Albuquerque
Rick Lowe,
Founding Director, Project Row Houses, Houston
Frieda Molina, MCP,
Manpower Development Resources Corp., San Francisco
Hon. Tom Murphy,
Mayor, Pittsburgh

Curits M. Davis

Lawrence Goldman

Min Kantrowitz

Rick Lowe

Frieda Molina

Mayor Tom Murphy

THE SELECTION PROCESS

The Selection Committee dialogue is at the heart of the Rudy Bruner Award. Each Selection Committee includes a mayor of a major American city and a diverse group of urban experts. Because there are no pre-established criteria for evaluating applications, the expertise and experience of the Selection Committee members are critical to the selection process. Each applicant must demonstrate what it considers to be its urban excellence, but it is Selection Committee members who discuss the projects and search for those aspects that make each case convincing. In so doing they create a framework within which all the projects can be judged, and they become part of a national dialogue on what constitutes an excellent urban place.

A new Selection Committee is appointed for each award cycle. The Committee meets twice: first to select the five winners from a field of about 100 applications, and then to select the Gold Medal Winner. Between these two meetings, Bruner Foundation staff research the finalists and then visit each one for two or three days, exploring the project and pursuing questions raised by the Selection Committee. These site visit teams serve as the Committee's eyes and ears. They tour all parts of the project, interview between 15 and 25 key participants (including "unofficial" participants and project opponents), take photographs, and observe patterns of use. Some of these activities are arranged by the project organizers, but the team members also pursue their own agenda in order to investigate the Selection Committee's questions and concerns. This year's site visit teams were led by Robert Shibley working with different co-authors

Mayor Murphy and Frieda Molina at the January meeting.

Lawrence Goldman and Curtis Davis review applications.

on each of the sites including Emily Axelrod, Jay Farbstein, and Rich Wener with Simeon Bruner as chief photographer.

After the site visits, the teams prepare site visit and reports and slide shows for the Selection Committee to digest when it meets again to review the five finalists in depth. With the site visit team leadership on hand to answer additional questions, the Committee then debates the merits of each project to decide upon a winner. In doing so, they explore the issues facing urban areas and come to a deeper understanding of the kinds of processes and places that embody urban excellence.

THE 1999 WINNERS

Gold Medal Winner

Yerba Buena Gardens, *San Francisco, CA*

Yerba Buena Gardens is a mixed-use development located in San Francisco's South of Market District. It includes an open space network with a 5.5-acre park, several high-profile museums, subsidized low-income and market-rate housing, a convention center, active commercial and entertainment complexes, and a wide variety of youth-oriented cultural and recreational facilities. By successfully integrating cultural, social, and economic development agendas, Yerba Buena has created not only a new destination in a formerly ailing part of San Francisco, but also a thriving neighborhood whose residents reflect the city's own diversity. Collaborative management practices bode well for the sustainability of this extremely complex enterprise.

Silver Medal Winners

ARTSCorpsLA, *Los Angeles, CA*

ARTSCorpsLA is a volunteer organization that has mustered the efforts of local inner-city Los Angeles communities to transform blighted parcels of abandoned land into public art places. The project includes three new LA parks and a series of murals throughout the city. It has creatively used art to involve many different segments of the community, particularly families and youth, and has used placemaking to strengthen connections between community members.

National AIDS Memorial Grove, *San Francisco, CA*

The AIDS Grove is a 7.5-acre park in the east end of Golden Gate Park. The Grove is a living memorial to the many thousands of victims of the AIDS epidemic in San Francisco. It is located in a formerly overgrown and derelict space known has the de Laveaga Dell, which it has reclaimed through volunteer labor and a unique public-private partnership. The AIDS Grove provides a much-needed place to publicly acknowledge and mourn losses from the AIDS epidemic, and for community building through monthly workdays and the ongoing maintenance program.

Parkside Preservation, *Philadelphia,PA*

Parkside Preservation is responsible for the restoration and re-use of dozens of elegant 19th-century homes bordering Fairmont Park in Philadelphia. Parkside has utilized creative financing tools to save the architecturally significant mansions, and has made historic preservation serve social needs by using the restored mansions as affordable housing and for social service agencies that serve the local community.

Portland Public Market, *Portland, ME*

A gift from benefactor Elizabeth Noyes and her philanthropic Libra Foundation, Portland Public Market has introduced a fresh food market into the Bayside neighborhood of Portland, thereby providing an important outlet for struggling Maine small farmers and providing an important new economic generator in the city's downtown. The attractive new building offers an inviting and transparent market environment that dramatizes the value of Maine agriculture, and draws in a variety of people from Portland and surrounding areas to shop, gather, and attend classes and events.

1999 AWARD PRESENTATIONS

Because the Bruner Award hopes to stimulate a national discussion of the nature of urban excellence in all its aspects, the Awards are presented in public celebrations designed to raise awareness of the winners' successes. Past Awards have been presented at the US Conference of Mayors, the US Department of Housing and Urban Development, and in a variety of winner cities. Planners, community organizers, architects, and developers speak about their projects, and mayors of winner cities are often present to commend the contributions made by winning projects.

This year, San Francisco Mayor Willie Brown hosted a press conference at Yerba Buena Center, where he spoke about the importance of both Yerba Buena Gardens and the National AIDS Memorial Grove to San Francisco. In a related event, Simeon Bruner presented the Awards at an evening reception that honored founders and participants in both projects. In Philadelphia, Mayor Rendell hosted a press conference to applaud Parkside Preservation, and Simeon Bruner hosted a panel discussion in which local, state, and federal officials discussed the tools available for creating affordable housing in Philadelphia. In Los Angeles, neighbors and families of the ARTSCorpsLA parks gathered to hear the places they had created receive national recognition. And in Portland the President of the Portland Public Market and of the Libra Foundation hosted a community-wide reception in which the Foundation and the Market were recognized for their unique and outstanding contribution to the revitalization of Portland.

Helen Sause of the San Francisco Redevelopment Authority

Director Thom Weyand, National AIDS Memorial Grove, with San Francisco Mayor Willie Brown

Award Founder Simeon Bruner with Philadelphia Mayor Ed Rendell

ABOUT THIS BOOK

In addition to the public Award ceremonies, the Bruner Foundation publishes a book containing case studies of the winners at the conclusion of each Award cycle. Each case study is prefaced by a "Project at a Glance" section that briefly summarizes the project. These overview sections are followed by detailed studies of the history, character, financing, and operation of each winner. In addition to describing the five winners, these case studies draw out the most important thematic elements that the Selection Committee recognized as constituting excellent urban places. Each case study thus recounts not only the story of the project, but the dialogue and debate the project provoked among Selection Committee members. After the five case studies, the contributions of each project to our understanding of urban excellence are then further explored in a conclusion that identifies and analyzes common themes.

From this year's winners, the Selection Committee derived a set of ideas and approaches that, when taken together, represent something larger than the sum of their individual parts. The elements listed below, all individually emphasized by the Selection Committee, were also considered to be part of a comprehensive, unified notion of "placemaking." Placemaking refers not only the physical construction and maintenance of places, but also to the quality of relationships between people and places as well as among the communities that make and use places. Its central premise is that making and caring for places – becoming committed to them – can be the basis for making and caring for communities. Excellence is achieved when good design comes out of a process that is sensitive to (and inclusive of) the human relationships in which it develops, and that, like a good guest, leaves those relationships better than it found them.

The Selection Committee identified the following as representative of some of the more persuasive elements of urban excellence in this year's winners:

- A commitment to a place, for what it could be but also for both its history and for what it is;
- An inclusive process that involves affected communities in a meaningful way, and thereby helps strengthen (or even create) the relationships that will use and maintain the resulting place;
- Incorporation of youth as an integral part of the process of making and using place;
- An animating vision that is both inspirationally committed to key elements and flexible enough to evolve in meaningful ways as it develops;
- A creative response that turns challenges, hardships, conflict, and even crises into opportunities;
- An effort to create the best possible place, not simply the minimum required by necessity;
- A work in progress that does not end when the place has been built;
- Effective leadership that energizes inclusiveness rather than dominating the process;
- Public-private partnerships that reveal how communities of place can transcend the political, economic, and cultural boundaries that hinder effective processes; and
- Creative and disciplined attention to project economics.

ABOUT THE AUTHORS

Robert Shilbley, AIA, AICP is a professor at the School of Architecture and Planning at the State University of New York at Buffalo. He is also the founding partner of Caucus Partnership, a consulting practice on environmental and organizational change. At the University at Buffalo, he is a former Chairman of the Department of Architecture and now serves as the Director of Urban Design Project, a center in the school devoted to the study and practice of urban design.

Emily Axelrod, MCP, is the Executive Director of the Rudy Bruner Award for Urban Excellence. She holds a Masters degree in City Planning from Harvard Graduate School of Design, and has worked in urban planning in both the public and private sectors in San Francisco and Boston.

Jay Farbstein, Ph. D., FAIA is an architect by training. He leads a consulting practice in San Luis Obispo, California which specializes in helping public sector and private clients develop and document their requirements for building projects as well as in evaluating the degree to which their completed buildings meet those requirements.

Richard Wener, Ph. D., an environmental psychologist, is head of the Department of Humanities and Social Services at Polytechnic University in Brooklyn, New York. He has done extensive research on the effects of built environments on individuals and communities.

BRUNER FOUNDATION PUBLICATIONS

Bruner Foundation books are currently in use in graduate and undergraduate programs in universities across the country. In addition, the work of the Rudy Bruner Award and its winners has been recognized by the US Conference of Mayors, the US Department of Housing and Urban Development, and the Environmental Design Research Association. Recent articles on the Award have appeared in *Foundation News, New Village Journal, Architectural Record, Casabella,* and *Design Book Review.* The program is also the subject of a book chapter in Robert Shibley and Lynda Schneekloth's *Placemaking: The Art and Practice of Building Communities* (New York: John Wiley & Sons, 1995).

Books from previous Bruner Award cycles, some of which are available from the Foundation, include:

1987
Philip Langdon with Robert Shibley and Polly Welch, *Urban Excellence* (New York: Van Nostrand Reinhold, 1990).

1989
Neal Peirce and Robert Guskind, *Breakthroughs: Re-creating the American City* (New Brunswick, NJ: Center for Urban Policy Research, Rutgers, State University of NJ, 1993).

1991
Jay Farbstein and Richard Wener, *1991 Rudy Bruner Award for Excellence in the Urban Environment: Connections: Creating Urban Excellence* (Boston: Bruner Foundation, Inc., 1992).

1993
Jay Farbstein and Richard Wener, *1993 Rudy Bruner Award for Excellence in the Urban Environment: Rebuilding Communities: Re-creating Urban Excellence* (Boston: Bruner Foundation, Inc., 1993).

1995
Jay Farbstein and Richard Wener, *1995 Rudy Bruner Award for Excellence in the Urban Environment: Building Coalitions for Urban Excellence* (Boston: Bruner Foundation, Inc., 1996).

1997
Jay Farbstein and Richard Wener, *1997 Rudy Bruner Award for Urban Excellence: Visions of Urban Excellence* (Boston: Bruner Foundation, Inc., 1998)

A recent Bruner Foundation endeavor has been to revisit the winners and finalists from the first four cycles of the award to learn how the projects have fared over time. Which have continued to thrive and which have struggled, and why? Partially funded by a grant from the US Department of Housing and Urban Development, teams of Foundation staff and consultants, HUD regional staff, and past Selection Committee members revisited 21 projects. The conclusions these observers reached has also been published, in a book available through the Bruner Foundation:

1987-93
Jay Farbstein, Robert Shibley, Polly Welch and Richard Wener, *Sustaining Urban Excellence: Learning from the Rudy Bruner Award, 1987-1993* (Boston: Bruner Foundation, Inc., 1998)

ACCESS TO OTHER RUDY BRUNER AWARD MATERIALS

All Rudy Bruner Award applications have been recorded on microfiche and are available through the Interlibrary Loan Department of the Lockwood Memorial Library at the State University of New York at Buffalo, Amherst, NY 14260 (Phone: 716-636-2816; Fax: 716-636-3721).

An abstract and keyword identification has been prepared for each application and can be accessed through two major databases: RLIN/Research Library Information Network and OCLF/First Search.

The State University of New York at Buffalo maintains a website with complete 1995, 1997 and 1999 applications for the Rudy Bruner Award:

http://wings.buffalo.edu/libraries/projects/digital/bruner

The work on this site is ongoing.

The Bruner Foundation also maintains a website on the Rudy Bruner Award for Urban Excellence:

http://www.brunerfoundation.org

The site contains an overview of the Award, visual images and summary information on all past winners, a list of past Selection Committee members, publications, information on how to apply for the Rudy Bruner Award, and brief profiles of each of the 1999 winners.

For more information, please contact:

RUDY BRUNER AWARD FOR URBAN EXCELLENCE

BRUNER FOUNDATION
130 Prospect Street
Cambridge, MA 02139
PH: 617.492.8404
FX: 617.876.4002

www.brunerfoundation.org

1999 Rudy Bruner Award

GOLD

medal winner

YERBA BUENA GARDENS

San Francisco, California

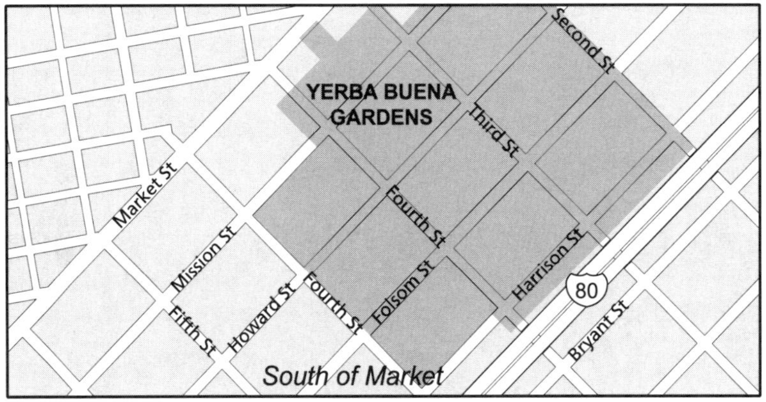
YERBA BUENA GARDENS
Second St
Third St
Market St
Fourth St
Mission St
Harrison St
Fifth St
Howard St
Fourth St
Folsom St
80
Bryant St
South of Market

San Francisco Bay
Golden Gate Bridge
San Francisco Bay Bridge
Presidio of San Francisco
80
Market Street
Golden Gate Park
SAN FRANCISCO
280
280

YERBA BUENA GARDENS AT A GLANCE

WHO MADE THE SUBMISSION?

- San Francisco Redevelopment Agency,
  Helen L. Sause, Deputy Executive Director.

WHAT IS YERBA BUENA GARDENS?

- Yerba Buena Gardens is an 87-acre urban redevelopment project in the South of Market (SOMA) district of San Francisco that includes a mixture of housing, open space, cultural facilities, children's facilities, a convention center, and commercial development.

Arts and Urban Amenities

- A world-class cultural community comprising more than two dozen museums and galleries, including the San Francisco Museum of Modern Art (SFMoMA), a Center for the Arts (CFA) complex, a Martin Luther King, Jr. Memorial, and a youth-oriented arts facility, "Zeum."
- A 10-acre complex of children's facilities including an ice skating rink and a bowling alley, a youth-oriented cultural center, an open space amphitheater and play/learning garden, and a 90-space child care center.
- A well-used cultural and artistic public space for SOMA locals and other San Franciscans centered around nearly six acres of public gardens.

Economic Development

- A wide range of rental and condominium residential facilities, including complexes for low-income seniors and working poor as well as market-rate units.
- A convention center supported by a mixture of hotels, commercial, and entertainment facilities.
- A highly popular destination for tourists from around the country and the world.
- Three high-rise office buildings.

Community Development and Social Justice

- A series of public-private partnerships that have reclaimed a neighborhood from the displacement caused by the "bulldozer" planning of 1950s and 1960s urban renewal.
- A network of stakeholder organizations that manage and sustain the project through continuous negotiation within and among different constituencies.

CHRONOLOGY

First Stage

1953
19.5 blocks in the South of Market area designated as a study area for redevelopment.

1953-1961
Redevelopment area shifted, becoming smaller (87 acres) and moving closer to Market Street. Design theme of convention center and sports-related facilities chosen.

1964
Livingston / Blayney and John Carl Warnecke produce preliminary concept and design plan, named Yerba Buena Gardens, for a "protected environment."

1966-1967
Yerba Buena Center officially designated an urban renewal area. In 1967 The Redevelopment Agency initiated demolition.

1967-1969
Kenzo Tange and then Gerald M. McCue and Associates chosen to produce the first plan for central blocks, based on the Livingston / Blayney and Warnecke concept. Request for developer proposals results in choice of Schlesinger/Arcon-Pacific.

1969-1975
Various lawsuits challenge dislocation, financing, and environmental concerns, including the successful 1970-1973 Tenants and Owners in Opposition to Redevelopment (TOOR) suit over the relocation process. Development was halted.

Second Stage

1976
Mayor Moscone appoints Select Committee to conduct public hearings and produce a consensus plan for central blocks. Resulting concept includes a public garden, subsidized housing, preservation of key historic buildings, and an underground convention center.

1978
Construction begins on Moscone Convention Center.

1980
Request for developer qualifications results in selection of Olympia & York. RFQ specifies land and financial exactions for public gardens and cultural institutions (Center for the Arts).

1981
The second master plan, Olympia & York's "Esplanade Plan," is selected.

1982
Moscone Center opens.

1984
Development and Disposition agreement reached with Olympia & York.

1985
James Stewart Polshek and Fumihiko Maki selected to design arts facilities.

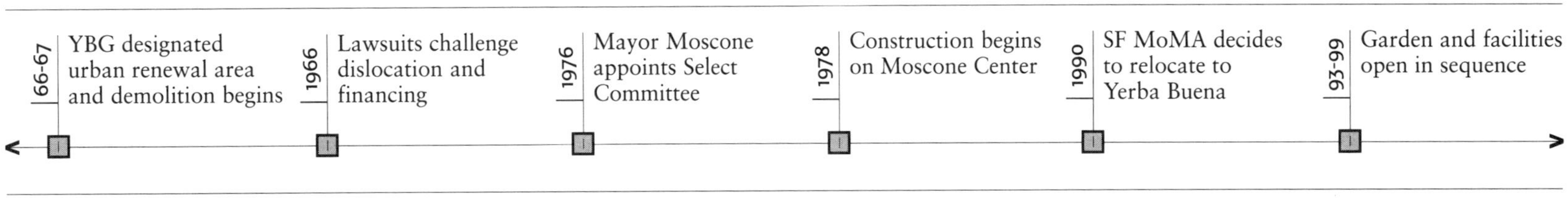

1986-1989
Marriott Hotel is constructed.
1989
Moscone Convention Center's two-part expansion under Central Block 2 and one-third of Central Block 3 begins.
1992
Olympia & York faces economic difficulties and is removed as lead developer.

Third Stage

1987-1990
San Francisco Museum of Modern Art decides to relocate to Yerba Buena.
1991
Yerba Buena Alliance formed. Central children's area, including ice rink, Childcare Center, and Zeum, planned.
1993
Gardens and Center for the Arts open. Moscone expansion completed.
1995
SFMoMA opens.
1998
Children's facilities open.
1999
Sony's Metreon opens.

KEY PARTICIPANTS

Individuals who were interviewed are marked with an asterisk [*]

City of San Francisco

Mayoral Administrations

Joseph Alioto (1967-1975)
George Moscone (1975-1978)
Dianne Feinstein (1978-1987)
Art Agnos (1987-1991)
Frank Jordan (1991-1995)
Willie Brown (1995-present)

San Francisco Board of Supervisors

* Supervisor Susan Bierman

Department of City Planning

Alan Jacobs, Former Director
* Hillary Gittleman, Major Projects

San Francisco Redevelopment Agency and Commission

* Helen Sause, Deputy Director and Project Director, Yerba Buena Gardens (1980-1997)
* Ed Ong, Chief Architect
* David Collins, former Project Director for Yerba Buena Gardens
* John Henry Kouba, SF Redevelopment Commissioner and Commission President
* Clifford Graves, former Executive Director
* William Carney, Project Director for Yerba Buena Gardens

Local Community and Nonprofit Groups

* John Marks, President, San Francisco Convention and Visitors Bureau
* Friends of the Garden
* TOOR (Tenants and Owners in Opposition to Redevelopment)
* John Elberling, Chairperson of the Consortium and Executive Vice President of TODCO (Tenants and Owners Development Corporation) and the Yerba Buena Consortium.
* Monsignor Fred Bitanga, Minister, St. Patrick's Cathedral
* Anita Hill, Executive Director; Matthew Witte, Chairman, Yerba Buena Alliance
* Mary McCue, General Manager, KTB Realty Partners
* Jeanne Nelson, President, Child Care Choices

Developers

* Mike Farrar, Millennium Partnership and Paula Collins, WDG Ventures (Sony Corporation's Metreon and the Market Street Four Season's Hotel)
* Jeffrey Snyder, Carpenter & Company and the Related Companies of California (3rd and Mission parcel developers)
* Hampshire, LLC (W Hotel at 3rd and Howard)
* Marriott Corporation

Architects

Kenzo Tange and Gerald McCue, architects of the first redevelopment plans

Ziedler Roberts Partnership, Willis Associates, Lawrence Halprin, Omi Lang, architects of the Olympia & York era master plan

James Stewart Polshek, Architect for the Yerba Buena Center for the Arts

Fumihiko Maki, Architect for the Center for the Arts Galleries & Forum

Mitchell Giurgola, Mallas & Foote, Omi Lang, Paul Friedberg, and Hargreaves Associates, designers of Garden / Esplanade

Mario Botta, Architect for San Francisco Museum of Art

* Cathy Simon, Principal, Simon Martin / Vegue Winkelstein Moris, architects for the Metreon
* Adele Santos, Adele Santos Architects, architects for the children's facilities

Pei, Cobb, Freed and Partners, architects of original 3rd and Mission office complex (redesigned as residential luxury apartments by Elkus, Manfredi Associates)

Arts Community

* William Osterhaus, Chair, Yerba Buena Policy Advisory Committee and Zeum Board Member
* Lori Fogarty, Senior Deputy Director and the new Director of Zeum
* John Killacky, Executive Director; Mario Garcia Durham, Performing Arts Curator, Yerba Buena Center for the Arts
* Mike McCone, Executive Director, California Historical Society

PROJECT DESCRIPTION

HISTORY

After a brief stint as a gold prospectors' camp in the mid-19th century, San Francisco's South of Market area evolved after the Civil War into an important service sector, geared largely to the city's port. Young, single, and often immigrant dock workers and merchant seamen formed a majority of the population, and industrial infrastructure and workers' housing came to dominate the landscape. As early as 1870, almost one-third of San Francisco's boarding houses and half of its lodging houses were located South of Market. The area's distinctive demographic pattern grew more pronounced over the following decades, reaching a peak when war workers flooded into the port during the 1940s. Building codes and aesthetic standards fell by the wayside as housing the massive influx of workers took first priority; temporary shelters and illegally subdivided apartments became the order of the day, dominating the South of Market area.

Needless to say, such developments did nothing to endear this working-class neighborhood to the city's elite, especially amidst the heady optimism of the postwar housing boom and urban renewal. In 1953, 19.5 blocks South of Market were designated a redevelopment zone by one of the nation's first redevelopment agencies. The area's fate was sealed in 1961, when changes in container technology shifted port activity to Oakland and deprived the neighborhood of its livelihood. By this time, city planners had begun to see the South of Market area as a promising adjunct to the financial district; the redevelopment zone accordingly migrated east and north toward Market Street, shrinking by nearly 10 blocks

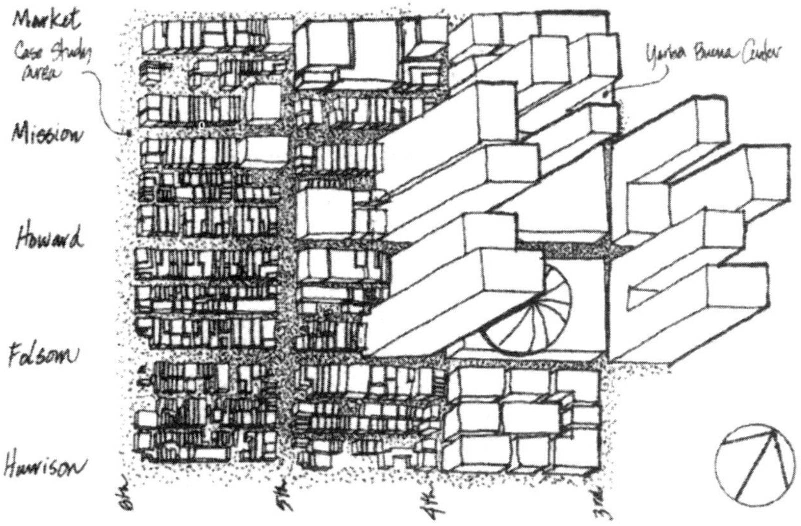

Early conceptions of Yerba Buena Gardens, (see for later scheme see p.16), envisioned a complex of high rise buildings in almost a fortress fashion. (Drawing reprinted by *Places* from Cheryl Parker's "Making a 21st-Century Neighborhood," vol 10 #1, 1995)

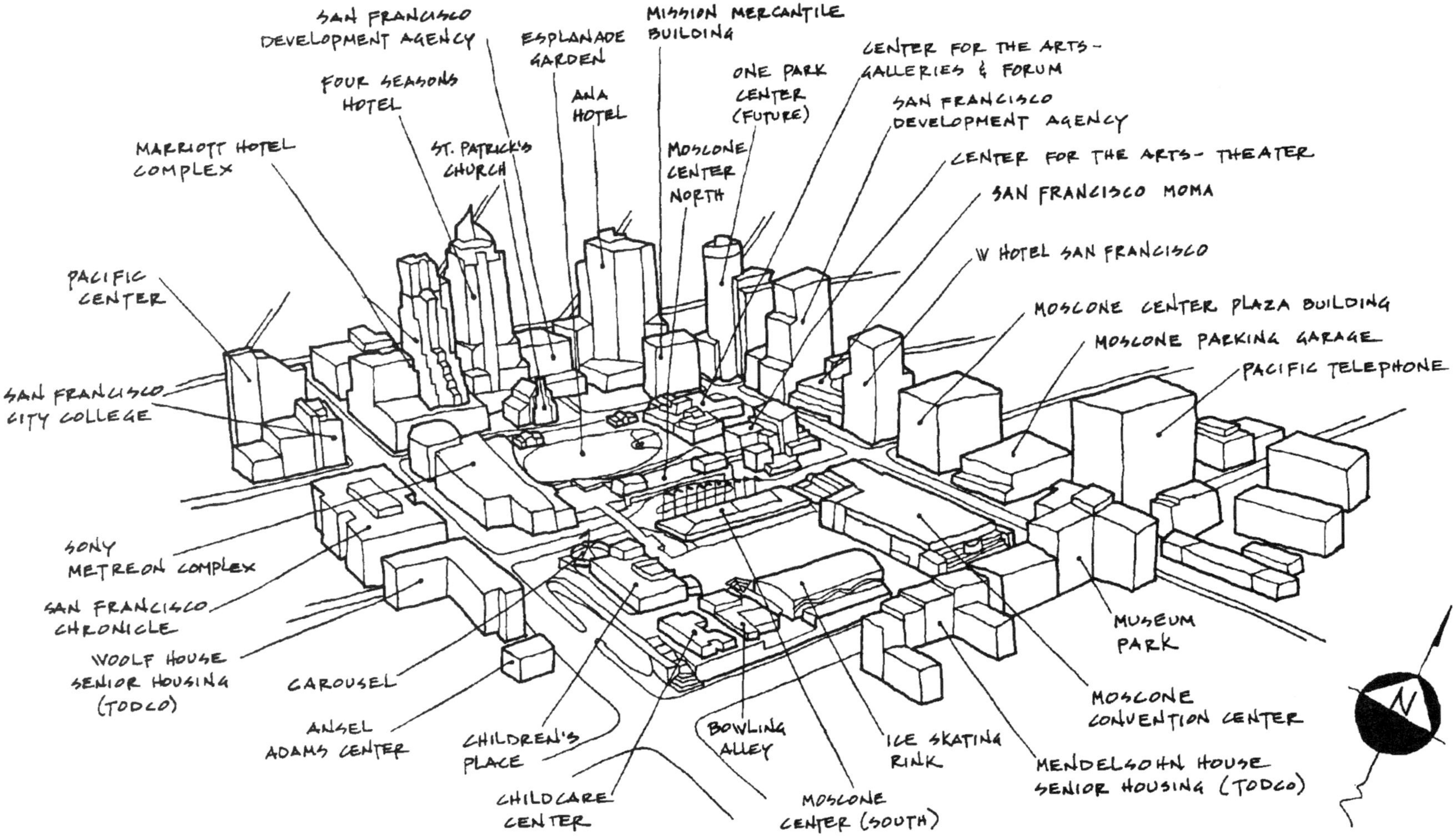

The diverse mix of land uses adds to the richness of the current Yerba Buena Complex.

along the way. For the next decade, conceptualizations of "Yerba Buena Center" featured large-scale commercial development – convention center, sports arena, theaters, a museum, office buildings, and retail – designed to promote gentrification of the surrounding areas.

These visions, however, ignored one crucial fact: approximately 4,000 people already lived in the South of Market area. To make room for Yerba Buena Center, their homes would have to be demolished. These residents, nearly all of them single, elderly, male, and poor, eked out a living on small pensions and Social Security; they seemed to have little defense against the federal bulldozer. According to historian Chester Hartman, a loose network of land-hungry planners, newspapers, and city officials used the area's poverty to depict it as a dangerous "Skid Row" ripe for redevelopment, populated by "bums" and "transients" whose fate mattered little. Like its cousins in other American cities, San Francisco's Redevelopment Agency acted with relative disregard for the local residents: it initiated mass dislocations, while planning only 276 units of new housing to replace the thousands of lost units.

After the demolitions, the grandiose redevelopment plan stalled. Indeed, little was accomplished under its auspices beyond the razing of several still-vibrant blocks South of Market. By the time construction was to have begun in the late 1960s, several factors had critically undermined the plan. Changes in corporate structure had shrunk the market for massive-footprint buildings; the Nixon Administration had weakened urban redevelopment agencies; and, perhaps most importantly, citizen resistance had grown in intensity and sophistication. Crucial in this last regard was a 1970 lawsuit filed by Tenants and Owners in Opposition to Redevelopment (TOOR). This group of low-income and elderly residents charged that the Redevelopment Agency had not met its legal obligation to provide housing for displaced residents. The settlement of the lawsuit forced the Agency to seriously re-evaluate its plans, and gave birth to Tenants and Owners Development Corporation (TODCO, a nonprofit housing developer). The lawsuit and citizen pressure forced the Redevelopment Agency into a new mode of planning, based on collaboration with neighborhood residents. The Agency's vision for the neighborhood – and its legally adopted and funded plans – now had to be rethought, and be achieved through negotiations, not by fiat.

Even after TOOR's success, the situation South of Market had hardly been resolved. As in many other American (and international) cities, urban renewal had left an ugly legacy. However, in San Francisco key lessons had been learned from the bitter legal battles, and when interest in redevelopment again picked up, it proceeded along very different lines. In 1976 San Francisco Mayor George Moscone appointed a Select Committee to study the area and produce a consensus design vision, explicitly encouraging citizen input through public hearings and discussions. This committee affirmed what were to be the most enduring elements of the project: the commitment to subsidized low-income housing (1,500 relocation rooms, plus 4 lots for TODCO to build new affordable housing); the goal of mixing a variety of commercial uses and public facilities; and, importantly, the idea of locating the convention center expansion underground and covering it with a public garden and other amenities. When the Redevelopment Agency sent out its request for qualifications, it emphasized another crucial aspect: it required developers to set aside land and funds for cultural institutions such as museums, exhibits, and theaters. In 1981, the Agency chose developer Olympia & York. All the elements of the modern Yerba Buena appeared to be in place.

Nothing in this project, however, was fated to be easy. Olympia & York suffered a long and painful decline over the next decade, finally concluding it could not proceed in 1990. Although the Marriott Hotel had already been completed by then, few of the developer's other plans were ever implemented. As it had with the lawsuit, however, the Redevelopment Agency turned this obstacle into an opportunity. Rather than seeking yet another single developer, it began to devise strategies for smaller scale developments within the project area that, in the end, were far more responsive to local conditions and needs than any one overarching template could have been. Still committed to the mixed use of retail, convention center, cultural institutions, low-income housing, and open space, the Agency shrewdly negotiated financial and design exactions from developers. These resources, combined with hotel taxes and the $34 million Olympia & York paid to buy out of its obligations, provided a foundation for the diversity of programs and uses that currently makes up Yerba Buena Gardens.

VISION

Since the convening of Mayor Moscone's Select Committee, the guiding vision for Yerba Buena has been that of a genuine neighborhood: a diverse mixture of different uses and constituencies co-existing in a new downtown community. The different constituencies – the arts community, the retail and commercial development, the convention center and tourist trade, and the housing needs of the lower income community – have been in bitter conflict at various times in the project's history, and have threatened to make development impossible. It was only when the Agency incorporated them into a single vision that Yerba Buena's greatest strength emerged: since power was distributed among the neighborhood's various constituencies, no single voice was able to dominate the process. With no one player able to achieve total control, development was forced to attend to the needs of all players. The result has been a balance of interests rather than a one-dimensional – and ultimately fragile – approach.

Balancing the diverse interests represented in the emerging neighborhood has resulted in development choices based on a broader vision than "highest and best use" for each particular plot of land, creating a complex layering of seemingly incompatible elements. The open spaces of the Esplanade Garden and the extensive areas devoted to child care and other youth amenities, chosen over more profitable commercial development, testify to the Agency's faith that Yerba Buena as a whole would be greater than the sum of its parts. The low-income housing, which might easily have continued to be a source of friction and resentment, instead became a centerpiece of the Agency's continuing commitment to inclusiveness. In particular, the Bruner Selection Committee was impressed by the efforts to include San Francisco youths. At a time when other urban entertainment districts and major urban redevelopment projects are discouraging youth from "hanging out," Yerba Buena actively invites them in. Bowling alleys, skating rinks, teen-oriented cultural facilities and creative electronic programming for older youth at Zeum are all there at a time when urban economics (especially San Francisco's) could easily have allowed for more profitable construction.

The inclusion of youth points to a more general commitment that Yerba Buena's cultural and commercial institutions be part of local as well as tourist life. The development was not intended to be a precious "cultural precinct" separate from the rest of San Francisco. Instead, the goal has been to integrate the project into the city, both architecturally and programmatically. Thus it is designed to be permeable at the edges (see "Urban Context" below), and the facilities are open to local use. Local residents are encouraged to put up shows at the Center for the Arts; fully one-third of the child care center spots are reserved for low-income neighborhood residents (with another third reserved for neighborhood businesses); and community folk often join the audiences of the many cultural events. Yerba Buena has seen the building of low-income housing, low-return childcare centers, and precious acres devoted to open public space at a time when other cities are focusing narrowly on visitors and tourist traffic. Ultimately, such decisions emanate from the vision of a genuine neighborhood, a place that gains value not only through tourist dollars but also from the opportunities and relationships it fosters for its own residents.

While remaining committed to this idealistic vision, the Agency did not ignore the bottom line economics or the aesthetics of the project. They ensured a healthy commercial life with diverse retail and entertainment venues, and selected internationally known architects to design a stylistic showcase of cultural and entertainment facilities. Their vision had always recognized the economic potential of the South of Market Area, and the introduction of social justice agendas after the lawsuits did not change that essential fact. Indeed, some of the most innovative aspects of the Agency's approach has been its ability to harness social justice goals to the engine of the neighborhood's profit potential in a variety of creative ways (see "Financing" below). This can be understood as having respect for what is actually present in a place rather than selecting or ignoring existing elements to suit a preconceived notion of what should be there. Simply because of location, among other factors, the potential for commercial development could no more be ignored or denied than the low-income population who so stubbornly refused to exit quietly. Both were elements of the neighborhood as it already existed, and plans for Yerba Buena were stymied until the inclusion of both became the Agency's vision.

ORGANIZATION/LEADERSHIP

At first glance, the story of Yerba Buena might appear to be about top-down leadership: the Redevelopment Agency, backed by land ownership, government power, and government money, learning through blunders and accomplishments on its way to ultimate success. The Selection Committee, however, found this appearance misleading. Certainly the project has been managed by top-down leadership, both to its benefit and detriment, but that leadership has been consistently shaped and modified by the local community. Faced with the common problem of recovering from the slash-and-burn urban redevelopment style of the 1950s and early 1960s, a diversity of stakeholders came together, sometimes combatively, in a process that eventually spoke to everyone's needs. Many extremely powerful players came to the table, but no single force dominated. Ultimately, the project's leadership would not be limited to City government, since many crucial elements of the plan originated in citizen pressure or the private sector.

Helen Sause of the San Francisco Redevelopment Authority.

The Redevelopment Agency

The main engine of Yerba Buena's development has always been the San Francisco Redevelopment Agency, which has managed the project for nearly four decades. Perhaps the single most important trait of the Agency has been its ability to adapt to changing circumstances, taking advantage of seemingly fatal obstacles to devise new and better strategies. In effect, the Agency has reacted to a series of legal and economic challenges by incorporating them into a broader and more diversified vision of Yerba Buena. The citizens' lawsuits, for example, taught the immensely powerful Agency that it could not ignore the people directly affected by its projects. The Agency was able to capitalize on its "defeat" and incorporate low-income residents and their housing into a new design concept. Later, the slow demise of Olympia & York weaned the Agency from its reliance on single-vision developers, introducing it to the crucial skills of piece-by-piece negotiation. In the long term, this produced a more responsive and participatory design process.

The site visit team was impressed that what could have been a story of frustrations, obstacles, and ultimate failure became instead a story of a vision shaped and tempered through difficult but ultimately fruitful interactions. The Selection Committee also recognized the strength of the project's episodic evolution, affirming that the process had been influenced by conflict over the years in positive ways – that conflict, in other words, had actually added value. The Committee saw evidence of *learning from*, not just *surviving*, this conflict in the wide variety of participants who say they are proud of the project. Everyone involved feels responsible (and wants to feel responsible) for what Yerba Buena has become. Since conflict will always be a part of urban settings, using it as a resource in this way instead of an obstacle is an important strategy. The Committee noted that credit is particularly due to the stewardship of Helen Sause, the deputy director of the Redevelopment Agency, for her skill at maintaining or rebuilding shattered relationships through this difficult process.

The Agency has repeatedly employed two innovative strategies since the 1976 Select Committee. The first was to wrest financial and design exactions from potential developers to maintain the project's funding and negotiated design priorities. Thus, for example, the lease revenues from the Marriott and Sony's Metreon are tied to profits, providing funding to maintain the Gardens and the arts complex. Buildings like Sony's Metreon and the 3rd and Mission Street project were redesigned to ensure their proper architectural "fit." All developers must look to locals as a "first source" employee pool, and many must participate in welfare-to-work programs. Access for disabled people had to exceed existing legal requirements (this predated the Americans with Disabilities Act). The public park had to include the historic carousel from Playland at the Beach, and historical photographs were designed into the Martin Luther King, Jr. Memorial in the plaza.

The various exactions also played a role in the Agency's second strategy, what one observer has called "client construction." For several of the key facilities – in particular, the Center for the Arts and the children's' cultural center (Zeum) – the Agency reserved space, earmarked operating funds, and actually began building long before there was a client to run the finished projects. Rather than selecting an existing organization to take over the facility, the Agency went to the community to develop its own institutions during construction, and then, after literally growing them to fit their tasks, encouraged them to form private nonprofit agencies. Given the length of time involved – more than 20 years – this strategy required an impressive consistency of vision.

Community Organizations

Community representatives explained emphatically to the site visit team that concessions were won from, not granted by, the Agency and the development process. Indeed, there is every indication that hard-fought battles attended nearly every major decision along the way, although most participants would agree that these battles ultimately strengthened the project, interjecting community perspectives into the process and educating the Agency about its role in the neighborhood. For example, an official at the child care center describes how local youths refused to back down on their request for a bowling alley, ultimately overruling the Agency with a carefully planned advocacy campaign. In fact, Yerba Buena's entire youth-oriented complex owes much to continuous pressure by local groups. The Selection Committee saw this narrative as crucial to the project's success, celebrating "how far we've come since the 1960s" by recognizing and awarding as Gold Medallists not just the Redevelopment Agency, but all contributors to Yerba Buena.

The battles over Yerba Buena have also spurred the creation of community organizations that have continued to advocate for residents as development continues. Thus TOOR, instrumental in strengthening and enforcing the City's legal obligation to provide low- and moderate-income housing in the early 1970s, became TODCO, a neighborhood-based nonprofit housing development corporation. TODCO prepared a 1981 master plan for the Yerba Buena Gardens Neighborhood, the only planning vision to flesh out the relationship between the central blocks and the residential area around them. The group helped form the South of Market Alliance to negotiate a "neighborhood benefits package" to be incorporated into the Redevelopment Agency's formal plan for the project. Some of the benefits negotiated included 300 units of low-and moderate-income housing in the surrounding blocks, "first source" hiring agreements for locals, ownership and operation of a significant portion of South of Market enterprises by neighborhood residents, and ongoing community participation in the planning process. TODCO has also developed four low-income housing projects and has been instrumental in advocating for the supermarket currently being planned by the Redevelopment Agency. Finally, the organization runs a community garden on a separate plot rented from the Redevelopment Agency for $50 per month.

Garden gate at TODCO's Mendelsohn House

St. Patrick's Church, one of the few historic buildings rescued from the bulldozers by neighborhood intervention, still serves the social outreach function it developed during the "Skid Row" years of the 1960s and 1970s, catering now to a mostly Filipino congregation. The church constructed Alexis, a 204-unit low-income housing project, as part of the post-lawsuit relocation strategy. Of more recent vintage, the South of Market Foundation grew out of coordination between existing community groups in 1990. The Foundation serves as an economic development contractor to the Redevelopment Agency, providing location and technical assistance, loan packaging, and other business-related services within Yerba Buena and the nearby earthquake recovery area.

Although determined to debunk any claims of magnanimity on the part of the Redevelopment Agency or the big developers, these community groups do have kind words for the way Yerba Buena has evolved, and for the opportunities it now offers neighborhood residents and institutions. Amalita Pascual of the South of Market Foundation notes, with some surprise, that local residents attend

Garden and art events. At St. Patrick's, Monsignor Bitanga's congregation spills out into the Gardens each week after church. The church's ethnic Filipino festivals also receive a boost from the Garden's facilities and high profile. Yerba Buena's youth programs also receive high marks: one-third of the child care center slots are subsidized and reserved for neighborhood kids; the CFA is open to local artists; and the extensive children's facilities provide programmed activities for local kids. Unplanned benefits such as the Metreon's Tai Chi Park and donations from the Marriott's periodic furniture stock renewals to St. Patrick's also emerged. Monsignor Bitanga's jokingly refers to Marriott as one of the church's "patron saints."

The Yerba Buena Alliance

The nonprofit Yerba Buena Alliance, formed in 1991, brings together all the area stakeholders including businesses, residents, hotels, cultural organizations, and public agencies. Its overall goal is to promote the neighborhood through media and community relations and community outreach. It also serves as an umbrella managing organization for the neighborhood, maintaining a healthy level of communication among the area's various constituencies through monthly meetings, monthly announcements, and a quarterly newsletter (*A New Leaf*). The Alliance is involved in most major aspects of Yerba Buena's daily functioning, from arts programming to economic networking. Importantly, they have also developed the capacity to gather political support from community groups to address shared concerns; for example, they led a campaign to stop a topless bar from moving into the area. Though they did not succeed, they were able to impose restrictions on its appearance and promotional activities. The Alliance's cooperative, inclusive structure sets the tone for other group dynamics in Yerba Buena, providing a model for the cultural community, maintenance and security organizations, and community groups.

DESIGN

Master Plans

The heart of the planning process has been a set of concepts present, in one form or another, since very early in the development. The notion of mixing commercial, convention center, and entertainment facilities, for example, has been present since the first master plan. The other key elements date primarily from the lawsuit and Mayor Moscone's Select Committee; these include the garden and its centrality, the cultural facilities, the youth accommodations and the low- and moderate-income housing. Although the specific formulations of these concepts have varied dramatically over the course of 45 years, five mayors, three master plans and their associated developers, and countless architects, the project has continued to be wedded to an enduring core vision.

The changing formulations of this core vision, however, have been an integral part of the story. The first plan, produced by Kenzo Tange and then Gerald M. McCue and Associates, was designed to connect the South of Market area to the financial district north of Market Street. To do this while providing a safe and hospitable zone for commercial development, Tange and McCue both proposed to divide the redevelopment area into central and peripheral blocks. The central blocks, featuring a convention center and a sports stadium, would be "protected" against the still "blighted" surrounding neighborhoods by the peripheral blocks, which would be a ring of high-rise office buildings. The developer, Schlesinger/ Arcon-Pacific, added Lawrence Halprin and Mario Ciampi to the McCue design team to flesh out the "urban fortress" plan. In hindsight, the plan's disregard for local residents stands out as one of its most salient aspects.

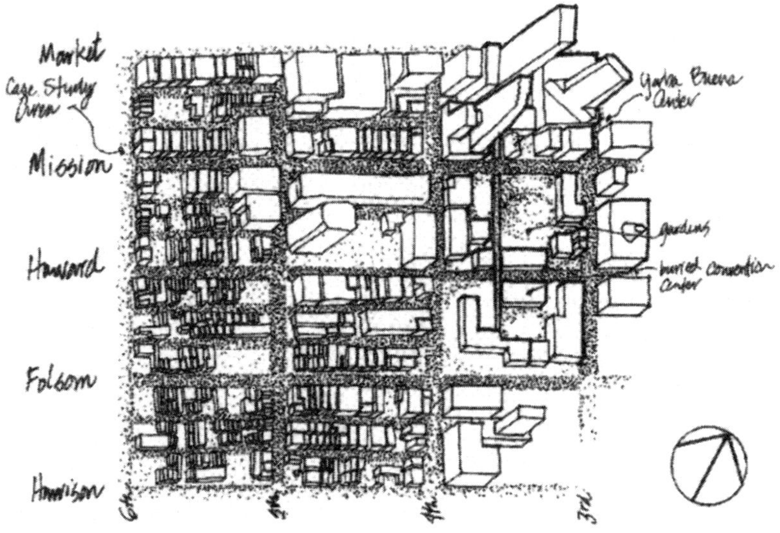

Over the years the Yerba Buena Gardens master plann began to soften the edges of the complex and open it to the surrounding neighborhood. (Drawing reprinted by *Places* from Cheryl Parker's "Making a 21st-Century Neighborhood," vol 10 #1, 1995)

It was this disregard that ultimately spelled defeat for the Tange-McCue plan amidst a welter of legal challenges in the 1970s. When interest again began picking up, the very first steps involved high-profile consultations with the public through Moscone's Select Committee and official recognition of TOOR through formal agreements about housing. The plan that emerged from this process relied heavily on the Select Committee's recommendations and TOOR's demands. Produced by developer Olympia & York with Agency and community oversight and designed by Zeidler Roberts Architects, the new concept centered around an open and inviting garden esplanade. The input of local residents (some legally enforced by the lawsuit) was evident in the expanded plans for low-income housing, and in agreements encouraging (and financing) TOOR to enter the housing development business itself. The cultural component resulted mostly from the suggestions of local artists invited into the planning process. Finally, commercial voices were by no means overshadowed amidst competing agendas, as the original vision of convention center, retail, office buildings, and entertainment complexes remained.

As Olympia & York's development capacity slowly fell apart in the 1980s, San Francisco's Redevelopment Agency cannily salvaged the key concepts from the ruins. In the process, it became ever more responsible on a day-to-day basis as the steward of good design and the mediator of different agendas. The Agency's selection of architects has been particularly strong, and its interventions during planning and construction have been effective. It is no accident that Yerba Buena has become a showcase for "new" architecture, boasting such famous names as Fumihiko Maki, James Stewart Polshek, Mario Botta, Mitchell Giurgola, and others on its buildings and landscapes. The Agency did not request proposals for specific buildings but instead chose architects based on a request for qualifications; conceptually, this approach meant a healthy diversity of designs, while practically it meant that the Agency could still exercise some influence over each design. And, importantly, the Agency was not afraid to wield this design influence, even when faced with powerful developers and talented architects.

Main Project Elements

Public Space

Yerba Buena's central gardens (the Esplanade) is the cohesive public element that ties the complex project together and connects it to the surrounding blocks. The Esplanade is a central open green space with simple planting. An extensive ramp and fountain system, capped by an overlook, relates surrounding restaurants and cafés to the green and performance areas and to a Martin Luther King, Jr., Memorial below. Entrances to the Metreon, the Visual Arts Center, and the Performing Arts Center all open onto the green, and SFMoMA's main entrance aligns with an east-west walkway that also joins the Center for the Arts to the Metreon. The park is well used, well maintained, and well suited to its passive functions as well as to the approximately 60 programmed events in the spring, summer, and fall of each year. The Esplanade was designed to accommodate small, intimate gatherings as well as performance art or public events drawing up to 5,000 people. The Selection Committee, however, questioned how well this balance has been

Looking across the main plaza toward San Francisco MoMA from the Metreon

struck, noting that the space is sparsely landscaped – perhaps favoring large public assemblies over smaller passive recreational uses.

Commercial Development

The 650,000-square-foot Moscone Convention Center is made up of an original building dating from the late 1970s, and a two-part expansion dating from the late 1980s. The two parts are quite different from each other, and both have been criticized in the architectural press for the way they relate to the surrounding streets. The original building is fairly typical of convention centers: a large box with a grand, welcoming front (north) flanked by three landscaped but essentially unfriendly exteriors (east, south, and west). Its design is fundamentally passive, and creates "dead" elevations on the surrounding sidewalks. The expansion,

North side of Howard Street entrance to the Moscone Convention Center with the esplanade and terrace above and to the left of the photo.

meanwhile, presents the key feature of the Convention Center, and a key element of the Yerba Buena master plan. At the insistence of Agency and community representatives, the expansion was put underground, thus reducing the structure's mass and impact, and allowing for more community-friendly uses such as the gardens and the Center for the Arts that sit atop it. From this point of view, the sinking was an unqualified success. The expansion has, however, received its share of criticism for street-level issues, particularly for the imposing service ramps that block foot traffic from the western side.

The Marriott Hotel was the first major commercial property developed, and is the only piece representing the Olympia & York era. Its size and location have helped make it one of the chain's highest performing hotels. The W Hotel, developed by Hampshire, LLC, opened in June 1999 on Third Street adjacent to SFMoMA. The first new hotel to open in San Francisco since the Marriott, the W is the flagship for the Starwood hotel chain. To help enliven Third Street, it includes an upscale street-level restaurant called XYZ. In addition, the Millennium Partners, working through their San Francisco associate WDG Ventures, is developing on Market Street between Third and Fourth the Four Seasons Hotel and Tower, a $400 million dollar project featuring a hotel and 142 high-end condominiums (at an average of 2,000 square feet apiece, they are slated to sell for $700 per square foot). Finally, Carpenter and Company's Third Street and Mission project will open in 2003 as a mixed-use building featuring a hotel, health club, African-American cultural center, and 95 high-end condominiums. Carpenter selected Skidmore, Owings, and Merrill as architects, although the Agency has reserved the right to give input. Since this is the last parcel of land in the area, the Agency conceives of this project as its last chance to influence the design character of Yerba Buena; in addition to the mixed-use theme, the building also highlights the area as a 24-hour neighborhood.

The Metreon, Sony's first large-scale urban entertainment center, is a five-story, $100 million, 350,000-square-foot entertainment colossus, and establishes the last built "edge" to Yerba Buena Gardens. Designed by Simon Martin-Vegue Winkelstein Morris, the Metreon faces the park on its west edge, and has extensive frontage on Fourth Street. The building's second floor entertainment

Metreon plaza entrance with the Marriott Hotel in the background

complex is sandwiched by retail tenants on both the first and third floors, and is anchored by an IMAX theater and a 15-screen cinema complex. Originally slated by WDG Ventures to be a multi-tenant building, the Metreon was unexpectedly leased in its entirety to an eager Sony Corporation, which uses it as an entertainment retail complex, showcasing its products. Sony was drawn to Yerba Buena by company policy – it was looking for downtown areas in transition with large site conditions – and by its recognition that San Francisco had nowhere to grow but South of Market. Getting there first, a company spokesman remarked, promised a variety of benefits. A confident Sony has projected more than 6 million visitors annually. Attendance thus far has exceeded projections.

Despite its size and high-powered finances, the Metreon has remained within the bounds of the Redevelopment Agency's vision. At the Agency's request, the building was redesigned (at a significant cost) to feature a 4-story atrium on the Garden side so that sunlight can still pass through to the Esplanade; the transparent walls also permit visitors to see and be seen from the gardens. Circulation links connect through the building to Fourth Street, where the somewhat unfriendly façade is softened by a number of pedestrian entrances (which also help lessen the impact of the Convention Center's service ramps). Sony is required to reserve a minimum of $1.35 million annually in contracts for women and minority-owned businesses. Finally, the Metreon helped secured the support of locals by providing a small park for seniors to practice Tai Chi.

Terrace entrance to the Center for the Arts designed by James Stewart Polshek

The Museums

Center for the Arts

The Yerba Buena Center for the Arts (CFA) consists of two buildings: a theater designed by James Polshek, and a galleries and forum building designed by Fumihiko Maki. The two parts share a single arts director. The CFA's mission is complex and diverse: it supports experimental and mainstream arts programs while remaining an accessible space for local art and performance projects. After one or two relatively lean years, the CFA has incorporated itself deeply into San Francisco's art scene. By two years it was already collaborating with six museums and 18 dance companies, and currently at least nine performance groups depend on it to guarantee advance booking. The use is fairly well balanced between local, experimental, and internationally known groups. At this point, five years after its opening, it appears to be succeeding in its mission, and has operated in the black every year.

Annually, 50 groups receive partial subsidies for performance work, 12 full subsidies for artists in residence are available, and three international groups make an appearance. Thus although the Center is open to local artists, performing or installing there is still a status-enhancing coup. Indeed, locals benefit from the guidance of the CFA staff, which offers technical and programmatic assistance to inexperienced groups.

The wide variety of constituencies served by the CFA has led one observer to describe the Center as a kind of "arts campus" available for museums, schools, and other institutions to use as a performance or gallery space, audiovisual studio, or whatever else they might need. The space has become so popular, in fact, it is somewhat at risk of degenerating into a mere rental facility without its own artistic vision. This tendency, however, has at least partially resulted from leadership issues that appear to have been resolved with the recent hiring of John Killacky. A proven arts administrator, Killacky has reaffirmed the CFA mission in regional and local arts promotion while ensuring its national and international reputation with a smart mix of programs.

San Francisco MoMA

The San Francisco Museum of Modern Art's (SFMoMA) presence at Yerba Buena was the result of a recruiting effort. In the late 1980s, the museum had outgrown its home on the third and fourth floors of the old war memorial building at the Civic Center. In 1987, the Redevelopment Agency approached the museum and asked it to join the Yerba Buena arts complex, sweetening its request by offering the land for just one dollar. Even so, it was a tough sell: Yerba Buena's arts complex was still a dream – the CFA would not open for six more years – and the area South of Market still retained its "Skid Row" reputation. Some SFMoMA board members claimed never to have even *been* South of Market; local wit offered Market Street as the dividing line between Northern and Southern California should the two regions ever separate. Nonetheless, SFMoMA made the move, locating its new signature building, designed by Mario Botta, on Third Street, and has never regretted its decision. In 1990, its first year at Yerba Buena, annual attendance quadrupled and membership tripled. As 800,000 visitors flooded the museum that year, it enjoyed some of the biggest months in its 60-year history. Indeed, some of these months were big by any standard: the SFMoMA rose to become the ninth most attended museum in the United States. As far as finances, it plans to receive revenue from its for-profit parking garage (which will provide the location and funds for a future rooftop sculpture garden), its café, and its museum store, which is reported by SFMoMA to be the most successful per-square-foot museum retail store in the nation. One explanation for the retail success is the small retail footprint and very dense merchandise displays. In light of these successes, it is fortunate that the building was designed to accommodate expansion, which is already being planned after only four years of operation.

Mario Botta's San Francisco MoMA with plaza fountain in the foreground

Zeum

"Zeum" is the name that eventually came to stand for the Children's Center for Technology and the Arts. Initially, the youth theme was pushed by an organization called Friends of the Gardens (FOG), a panel of community advocates and representative city organizations that dates back to the Mayor's Select Committee. After securing a large federal grant, Zeum gained more focus and carved a niche for itself as a studio for technology and the arts targeting older youth. This facility is arguably the crown jewel of the youth-oriented facilities (see "Other Children's and Recreational Facilities" below).

These three anchors — CFA, SFMoMA, and Zeum — form the heart of the arts community. More than just physical proximity brings these facilities together; like the project as a whole, the arts scene depends on cooperation and coordination among its various parts. On a large scale, this has been the province of the Yerba Buena Alliance, whose yearly Gardens Gallery Walk brings 5-10,000 art admirers to experience Yerba Buena's cultural scene, which also includes 20 or more smaller art galleries that have located in and around the central blocks. In all, the Garden hosts about 60 free art performances per year, with attendance averaging 5,000 per event.

But the arts community does not exist solely at such grand levels. Indeed, smaller details are even more revealing of the extent of interdependency among the various facilities. For example, when the SFMoMA closes on Wednesdays – instead of the more usual Mondays – it leaves a sign directing visitors to the CFA; tellingly, Wednesdays are the CFA's highest volume days. Correspondingly, when the CFA is closed on Mondays a sign points visitors to the SFMoMA. The SFMoMA uses the CFA's theater as its presentation house, particularly useful for educational programming. The museum has also developed a good synergy with the nearby California Historical Society. Materials are borrowed back and forth, and occasional companion shows link them directly. Tickets

Zeum interior video installation

to SFMoMA are good at the Historical Society, and 25% of the Historical Society's new audience can be traced to this nicety.

All of this intensive joint activity has had an impact on the city as a whole. Officials at SFMoMA have noted an increase in citywide arts cooperation. SFMoMA and the CFA have taken part in shared shows or exchanges with the de Young Museum and the Asian Art Museum located elsewhere in the city. At the financial level, San Francisco's arts community was knit together under the pressure of the "tax-revolt" Proposition 13. Instead of competing with each other for City funding, all the arts groups got together and fought for a share of the city's hotel tax dollars, which they then divided up cooperatively among themselves (40% for the big institutions, 60% for the small ones). This strategy helped make funding clearer to businesses interested in helping the arts. In an unusual move, San Francisco's hotels actually approached the City and requested an increase in their bed taxes to help support the arts.

Other Children's and Recreational Facilities

In addition to Zeum, the Rooftop at Yerba Buena features an historic carousel, a bowling alley, an ice skating rink, a child care center, and a children's garden, all of which are on top of the original Moscone building. Designed by architect Adele Santos, the structures are painted in striking colors – mauve and yellow-orange, for example – and employ a sensuous, curvilinear geometry toward the inside of the block. The buildings feature many appropriately child-scaled features such as lowered windows. Again the Selection Committee affirmed the importance of making a designed-for asset, especially when most other entertainment and retail complexes of this type are trying to keep them out.

The roof top play area on top of the Moscone Convention Center

The historic carousel relocated from San Francisco's Playland-at-the-Beach

Housing

TODCO has developed four housing projects that provide space for about 1700 low-income, disabled, and elderly residents. Three of the six buildings, holding 500 households (approximately 700 tenants), are in Yerba Buena Center proper. Seventy-five percent of the residents are elderly or have disabilities, 20% are African American, 40% are Chinese American, 20% are Filipinos, and the remaining represent a mixture of other cultures and ethnicities. Rents are subsidized, ranging from 30% to 40% of household income. The Woolf Houses I, II, and III (212 units) were completed in 1979, 1982, and 1996 respectively; Ceatrice Polite Apartments (91 units) in 1984; the design award-winning Mendelsohn House (189 units), designed by local architect Bob Herman in 1988; and the Leland Apartments (24 units) in 1997. The funding for these buildings came from a variety of sources: the Woolf Houses were built with funds from the California Housing Finance Agency; Ceatrice Polite is a HUD building; and Mendelsohn depended upon trustee and City (hotel tax) money. The buildings are managed by an outside company, but TODCO stays in close contact with tenants through a variety of services such as arts workshops, exercise and recreation classes, nutrition and wellness programs, and counseling. A licensed residential care facility with 150+ units is in the works.

Beyond the TODCO homes, the diverse housing mix ranges from the Yerba Buena Commons SRO project, which caters to low-income hospitality workers, to the approximately 1,500 market-rate units (20% of which are subsidized for low- and moderate-income residents), to the Four Seasons' high-end condos. Providing

TODCO's Mendelsohn House on Folsom Street

Community garden plots for local residents on land permanently secured by the San Francisco Redevelopment Agency

housing for a range of income levels and household characteristics is very much a part of the vision for Yerba Buena as a new downtown neighborhood.

Streetscape

While several well-known architects are associated with the buildings of Yerba Buena, both the site visit team and the Selection Committee agreed with a critique leveled by the professional press and identified in Yerba Buena's own award application: architecturally, the project presents a mixture of significant accomplishments that have not been perfectly integrated to create a unified place. Thus, impressive elements like the buried Convention Center, the extensive list of high-stature cultural facilities, and the striking architecture of buildings like the SFMoMA coexist with missed opportunities at the streetscape level, particularly on Third Street and in some of the public spaces created by the buildings on the esplanade.

URBAN CONTEXT

Edges

Yerba Buena is bounded by high-end downtown retail and the financial district to the north; a mixed neighborhood of families, transients, retail, and light industrial space to the west; a developing area being taken over by offices and retail to the east, and two main freeways to the south, beyond which is the future site of the new baseball stadium in the China Basin. It is thus on the way from and to major destinations in three directions, especially between the freeways and downtown.

Efforts have been made to connect the development area to its neighbors. Pedestrian walkways, for example, criss-cross Yerba Buena along the north-south and east-west axes; a BART (Bay Area Rapid Transit, the regional transit system) station will open soon at the Four Seasons Hotel & Tower; and visually, the low-profile convention center and the few high-rises present a relatively soft border to adjacent neighborhoods. The Selection Committee felt, however, that these nearby residential areas could in fact have been better connected to the Garden: while the project's current edges are far more permeable than the barricade-like boundaries featured in the original Tange plan, a dramatic difference remains between the new cultural and entertainment area and surrounding residential blocks. The Committee did see reason to expect improvement in this regard, particularly through the as-yet-unfinished pedestrian walkways. Ultimately, for an area as intensely developed as Yerba Buena, the project is surprisingly well integrated into the city.

A Pedestrian's-Eye View

Of Yerba Buena's unresolved streetscape issues, none is more important or vexing than Third Street. Originally intended to be a service street at the edge of the project, Third Street has become a central part of the project and is the main entrance to the SFMoMA. The hotels flanking the SFMoMA were not complete as of our site visit (though the "W" has since opened), and though they promise further street-level attractions (for example the XYZ restaurant, which has also opened since our visit), their eventual impact on the streetscape is difficult to determine. As of our site visit, the west side of the street, which forms the eastern edge of Yerba Buena, was basically a blank wall burdened by service entrances to the Performing Arts Center and the Visual Arts Center. While this lifeless frontage is ameliorated to some extent by SFMoMA's café and bookstore across the street and the East Garden, the axis between the CFA and SFMoMA across Third Street is a major access point that unfortunately feels like an afterthought.

Other street-level problems are less stark. Despite landscaping, the Convention Center makes a relatively sterile edge on the south and west perimeter of the project leading up to the Metreon on Fourth Street. The Metreon itself, however, allows foot traffic through to

The Third Street facade of James Polshek's Center for the Arts has been criticized for the blank wall it presents to the street.

the interior of the Gardens, and the Tai Chi park and commercial frontage break up the building's monolithic street edge on Fourth Street. The facade above the first floor also provides variation with eye-catching cinema bays and the IMAX screen on the corner of Fourth and Mission. The Mission Street facade north of the Garden is the most open to the street, featuring multiple ways into the Garden, good sight lines from the Garden out to St. Patrick's Church, the future Jewish and Mexican Museums, the Marriott, and the new Four Seasons Hotel on Market Street. A pedestrian spine is under construction that will link Market Street to Yerba Buena, threading through the garden and leading over the convention center along the way to the children's facilities. This pathway is designed to be a major pedestrian connector leading to the central block. It will be marked on Market Street with an entrance adjacent to as well as through the Four Seasons Hotel now under construction, and will eventually be fully landscaped and framed by commercial activity.

Parking and Traffic

The Agency has been especially attentive to the potentially calamitous transportation consequences of such a large, sensitively located development. Consistent with City policy, but not always with the concurrence of project developers, there has been a conscious decision to limit parking while promoting mass transit use, improving the pedestrian experience, and providing an extensive bicycle system. Thus, for example, the 2,600 car garage at Fifth and Mission streets has sacrificed 55 parking spaces for a ground-level retail complex to make its street edge friendlier. The area's parking fees are structured to discourage long-term commuter parking (rates go up after the second hour). Pedestrian walkways, talking street signs, widened sidewalks, timed signals, red light cameras, and mid-block traffic lights will all help make walking an attractive option.

MAINTENANCE, OPERATIONS AND SECURITY

One of Yerba Buena's more impressive aspects is the smoothly coordinated day-to-day management of the complex. The Redevelopment Agency contracts with KTB Realty Partners, Inc., a private property management firm, to manage the maintenance and security in close collaboration with the arts programmers. The Selection Committee was pleased with the cooperative management dynamics developed between these organizations and other interests outside the formal property boundaries of Yerba Buena. KTB issues permits for use of the public spaces for all planned organized events, of which there are between 67 and 100 per year, ranging from the "TODCO poets" to the San Francisco Opera. This requires more than just careful scheduling. KTB works with arts programmers to ensure that the space isn't "overactivated," turning visitors into passive receptors of recreation. Event organizers work with KTB's Mary McCue and the CFA's Mario Garcia Durham to develop their programs and get permits. All outdoor events are free, and permits, while required for just about anything, are fairly easy to get. Four times a year the entire space can be rented out for private functions; the lease revenue provides funds for the free public programming.

Security arrangements are anchored by a "faces with places" program, in which the security personnel of all the buildings around the Gardens – public and private – meet every two months to share security information and concerns. Because of this coordination, Yerba Buena's facilities all share a single, efficient central dispatch (it once was the first to respond to a call from St. Patrick's). Their cameras also operate together to form a comprehensive network. Finally, security and maintenance workers are familiar with the area, are available to offer help for visitors and, on occasion, to appear in public performances. This friendly style is further embodied in rules allowing people to sleep on the grass or even on the benches when the area is not crowded; also, people are generally not asked to leave. Individual vendors, however, are not allowed, and panhandlers are asked to get a permit. Overall, the security program is so successful that Mary McCue is a sought-after instructor, teaching about the arrangements to staff at Oakland's City Center, San Francisco's Union Square and Civic Center, and Philadelphia's Independence Square.

FINANCES TABLE

Project	Size	Units	Cost ($ mil)	% Public	LDA	Exaction	Amount	Use
Moscone Convention Center (with expansions)	1.3 Million sq. ft.	N/A	330	100%	Purchase	20 years of rent payments	$896,000 annually	
Marriott Hotel	1.9 Million sq. ft.	1500 rooms	300	0	Lease	Lease payments tied to profit		Rent used for CFA maintenance and gardens operations
Esplanade Garden	5.5 acres	N/A	40	100%				
Center for the Arts	100,000 sq. ft.--three galleries, video screening room, multipurpose forum, 775-seat theater	N/A	40	100%				
Children's facilities	34,000 sq. ft. Zeum 32,000 sq. ft. Ice skating/Bowling 10,000 sq. ft. Child Care Ctr 130,000 sq. ft. Outdoor Space	N/A	58	100%				
Metreon	350,000 sq. ft.	N/A	100	0	Purchase	Welfare-to-work first source agreement		
SFMoMA	225,000 sq. ft.	N/A	65	0	Purchase			
W Hotel	305,450 sq. ft.	423 rooms	73	0	Purchase	Welfare-to-work first source agreement Hunt Lane open space	$700,000	half the cost for pedestrian walkway
Four Seasons Hotel & Tower	750,000 sq. ft.	250 hotel rooms 270,000 sq. ft. condos.	350		Purchase	One-time payment welfare-to-work first source agreement childcare fee affordable housing fee contribution to security, operation, and maintenance of CB-2	$2 million $750,000 $2 million 160,000 annually	
Third and Mission Street Project NE Corner	492,000 sq. ft.	500 Units	129	Bond financing	Purchase	Affordable housing fee. Childcare fee	$2.6 million, $492,000	20% units for low income
TODCO housing								
Woolf Houses I, II, III	150,000 sq. ft.	212	14	100%				
Ceatrice Polite Ap'ts	79,445 sq. ft.	91	8	100%				
Mendelsohn House	151,000 sq. ft.	189	15	100%				
TOTAL	**11.4 mil. sq. ft.**	**2995**	**15.2 billion**				**9.6 million**	

FINANCING

The Redevelopment Agency has been shrewd and creative in its efforts to secure funding for the project without sacrificing its vision. This has involved relying on a wide variety of funding sources. Thus tax increment financing, land sales, the City's hotel tax, private developer investment, and exactions have all played important roles in keeping Yerba Buena moving forward and in creating its richness and programming.

In addition to the obvious advantage of owning all the land, a two-part strategy has guided the Agency's pursuit of funds. First, they invested energy and significant public dollars into planning the land to make it worth more, and then used the profits from that added value to pay for the planned improvements and operations. The crucial element here was the Garden, plans for which raised land values enough to provide $26 million in tax increment funds. In turn, the promise of the Garden gave the Agency leverage in the second of the two major strategies, exacting funds from private developers to invest in the cultural and youth facilities and the open space. In short, the Agency put forward a vision for Yerba Buena and then banked on it, parlaying its own faith in future development into funding from developers.

PUBLIC-PRIVATE PARTNERSHIP

A consistent theme that stands out in the narrative of Yerba Buena is the delicate web of relationships that have evolved between the City of San Francisco and the neighborhood's various private stakeholders. The most striking example is the role of private nonprofit housing developers like TODCO and St. Patrick's Church. The powerful narrative of TODCO's transformation from opponent to collaborator has been institutionalized in current arrangements, in which the community group is responsible for carrying out the Agency's legal obligation to provide low-income housing in Yerba Buena. That a private developer would be selected to undertake this responsibility may be no surprise; that such a selection would be used to meaningfully incorporate the Agency's one-time implacable foe is emblematic of this project's democratic creativity.

The agreements with TODCO were not the Agency's only public-private partnership. The Yerba Buena dream could also not have been achieved without the exactions agreed to by major private players like the Marriott and Sony (see "Finances" chart and

Plaza entrance to the Center for the Arts

"Leadership" above). Those private developers would probably not have been so eager to join Yerba Buena if the City had not made serious commitments to the location through quality planning and extensive additions to the transit infrastructure. Both sides, clearly, were willing to make extra investments to make the project work. Developers accepted extra costs and design complications, and the City only demanded exactions that had specific value for the Yerba Buena concept.

This self-interested but unselfish commitment to Yerba Buena's overall goals also appeared in what is surely the most innovative of the Redevelopment Agency's strategies, the "client construction" that created private organizations to run several key art facilities (see "Leadership" above). Here, the Agency served as a nursery for private institutions, crafting them carefully within the protected space of public ownership until they were prepared to pursue their mission as private nonprofits. Underlying these transactions is the assumption that the private and public sectors are not opponents, nor is one the simple handmaiden for the other; rather, both must work together as crucial contributors to a larger agenda. This spirit of cooperation and compromise, embedded in the concrete deals struck between the Agency and Yerba Buena's developers, make the project a hopeful model that other cities could do well to emulate.

IMPACT ON THE CITY

San Francisco has reaped a number of benefits from Yerba Buena. Aesthetically, it has raised its worldwide stature by becoming a showcase for the giants of "new" architecture. In social terms, key developments include an improved commitment to low- and moderate-income housing in the downtown area, increased cooperation within the city's arts community, and the enlivening of the downtown financial area. Politically, the City and Redevelopment Agency will leave this project extremely well educated in the process of urban renewal; this knowledge will hopefully serve them in good stead as they turn their efforts to the earthquake recovery area to the west of Yerba Buena and the redevelopment area to the east. Also, the development of viable political organizations at the neighborhood level, if sustainable, bodes well for future efforts to renew or reclaim troubled areas. Further, Yerba Buena's economic impact is considerable. Beyond bringing in tourist and tax dollars, the project has shown a

Skating rink with view of downtown in background

promising ability to generate jobs. And, perhaps most importantly, the exaction process has provided a model for how cities can entice business development without submitting to a one-way courtship of high-cost corporate giveaways.

FUTURE PLANS

Several large-scale building projects are on the immediate horizon. The Four Seasons and the hotels on Third Street are under construction. The Convention Center will expand again soon behind the Fifth & Mission garage, and SFMoMA also has plans to grow. TODCO's next project is a licensed residential care facility with 150+ apartments slated for the year 2000. Additionally, a 494 unit apartment building on Third and Mission that began construction in August 1999; 100 of its units are for low- and moderate-income tenants.

A number of transportation improvements are also in the pipeline. Most importantly, a light rail transit link is planned to China Basin and the new baseball stadium; it will be above grade several blocks south of Yerba Buena, then go underground beneath downtown to Chinatown and points north. Public transportation enhancement will be supported by improved pedestrian and bicycle pathways, most notably the walking path that will link Market Street to Mission Street through the garden and past the Convention Center.

In general, the Selection Committee felt that prospects for sustainability were very good. Exactions from the development process have taken care of the basic infrastructure and overhead of the arts complex, making it easier for the cultural facilities to fulfill their double role as profitable institutions and as accessible venues for local and internationally known artists. Also, the Committee noted that the project's diverse group of stakeholders provides a healthy system of checks and balances for future development. Yerba Buena presents itself as a work-in-progress: while most of the big construction has been completed, fine tuning of the general character, management, and public spaces will doubtlessly continue well into the future.

ASSESSING PROJECT SUCCESS

HOW WELL PROJECT MEETS ITS OWN GOALS

- *To reclaim a previously marginalized sector of the city.*

Yerba Buena has made great progress toward accomplishing this goal. Economic activity South of Market has increased astronomically, cultural life is thriving, the housing ills are being addressed, and land values have continued to rise. As Monsignor Bitanga put it after his return to the area in 1994, the difference was obvious: "more clean clothes," he explains, "and fewer street people." While there is clear evidence of gentrification, the success of TODCO and of other housing providers (including the Salvation Army) has put an end to mass displacement. The area has a diverse mix of rich and poor and enjoys broad ethnic diversity.

- *To provide employment, children's facilities, open space, cultural facilities, and other amenities to its citizens.*

The children's facilities, open public space, cultural facilities, and other amenities like the Tai Chi park and the skating rink testify to Yerba Buena's success in meeting this goal. Job creation has been more challenging; as could be expected, there are serious obstacles to overcoming this entrenched problem. Although the number of jobs has gone up in the area, many of them require more training than local residents have. Nonetheless, given the nature of the employment dilemma, one would have to characterize the advances on this front as hard-won and significant.

The gardens present a variety of small-and large-scale planted areas.

- *To support the growing tourism industry.*

The growth of hotel rooms in the area, the increased number of events enabled by the expanded convention center, the mix of regional and international art venues, and Sony's newly opened Metreon have all helped to make a substantial new place for repeat tourist visits even while it attracts local populations. Yerba Buena Gardens is clearly supporting San Francisco's bid for a still larger share of the world's tourism economy.

OTHER MEASURES OF SUCCESS

Impact on Neighborhood and Community

Yerba Buena's impact on its physical and social context is undeniable. In most instances, it has meant an improved quality of life. The site visit team observed that the proliferation of art galleries, restaurants, theaters, museums, entertainment facilities from the Metreon to the bowling alley, and of simple public open space have all made the area a lively, busy place. The youth-oriented facilities have given local young people alternatives to just "hanging out." The emerging focus on pedestrian, bike, and mass transit usage will help make this new liveliness appear on a human scale rather than manifesting itself in traffic jams. The physical connections provided by Yerba Buena's crisscrossing walkways and alleys have done much to improve the physical connectedness of the area as a whole. Finally, the opening of the BART station and the planned light rail to the area (possible in large part because of Yerba Buena's traffic draw) will mean a greater incorporation into the city's regular rhythms of day and night life. In all, the Selection Committee, many of whom were familiar with Yerba

Buena, confirmed the feeling that this was an ambitious, active, successful, "more-than-one-visit kind of place."

The neighborhoods near Yerba Buena have seen fewer direct benefits. The intense attention and funds directed at Yerba Buena could easily have fostered a feeling that the surrounding neighborhood has been left out. Indeed, some locals do offer pointed observations in this regard. Criticisms, however, often sound more like "you should be doing that where I live too," instead of actual disagreement with planning decisions. Beyond this, neighborhood advocates do acknowledge Yerba Buena's positive impact. In addition to their participation in the cultural and entertainment scene, residents of the surrounding areas benefit from the mass transit upgrades and, not least, from the changed nature of the "new-look" Redevelopment Agency. The Agency has already declared itself more interested in preserving historic buildings as it turns its attentions to the east and west of Yerba Buena, and is proceeding under the displacement laws established by the TOOR suit. As renewal of the surrounding areas unfolds, it is safe to assume that it will be a better, less oppressive process because of the lessons of the 1970s.

Finally, the development process has played an important role in creating and then fostering neighborhood political self-awareness and organization. Groups like TODCO, the South of Market Alliance, the South of Market Foundation, the Yerba Buena Alliance, and the "faces with places" security group represent concrete examples of community identity. These organizations are crucial to the coordination of this complex urban ecosystem on a short- and long-term basis. They also provide what has always been necessary in the "real" world of urban finance and development: the political muscle to make sure their community's voice is heard even alongside such colossi as the Millennium Partners, Sony, and the Redevelopment Agency. Only through the vigilance and advocacy of these kinds of organizations can Yerba Buena continue as an entity committed to the needs of multiple constituencies.

Values Reflected in Development Process

The values that sustain Yerba Buena Gardens today are fundamentally democratic. The project has depended on good leadership and a lengthy process of development that in the end has left room for the negotiation of conflict in a manner that is flexible and inclusive. The core of this democratic process has been a commitment to the neighborhood and its promise, and a willingness to accept that it must be shared. Every major player has had to make significant tradeoffs of one sort or another. The leading example of this has been the Redevelopment Agency itself, which abandoned its dream of a giant development that would bear the imprimatur of a single great urban innovator, accepting instead a smaller role and shared credit. In short, rather than following a single agenda, Yerba Buena has developed along the lines of an actual neighborhood: messy, at times fractious, but also vibrant, self-correcting, and, at the best of times, a true community.

It was the impressive diversity of this functioning community that originally interested the Selection Committee in the project, though they were skeptical that a development so big could truly succeed in paying attention to process and social justice. Yerba Buena's rare openness to diverse populations and uses, however, persuaded the Committee that the "big must be bad" cliché had indeed been debunked. In a nation full of bad examples, the Committee noted, here is one large urban intervention that "got it right."

The Selection Committee generalized three exportable lessons for the Yerba Buena experience:

- *Strong leadership is important to develop and sustain a core vision while remaining open and flexible to change.*

Yerba Buena has succeeded in no small part due to the strong leadership of the SFRA, TOOR, and its successor TODCO. They developed a sturdy core vision of a mixed-use commercial, office/ convention center, entertainment, and cultural complex. This consistent core vision, importantly, has served as a foundation for flexibility. Valuable later additions like the Gardens, low-income housing, and youth-oriented facilities added significantly to the richness and complexity of the project. Once incorporated, these later concepts became part of the project's core vision, stubbornly adhered to for nearly two decades. As a result, the Agency proved that a good development vision can be a solid basis for attracting commercial development – a basis ultimately cheaper and more productive than direct payoffs in the form of tax breaks, free land, and so forth. A good development vision can also sustain a project through changing political climates; Yerba Buena survived five mayoralties, each with a different idea of how to proceed. These successes, the Selection Committee felt, depended upon having a consistent vision that nonetheless could be reshaped in response to ongoing community concerns. As one Selection Committee member remarked, they were willing to change but "didn't throw the baby out with the bathwater."

- *Conflict adds value to the project.*

Although the first lessons in this education were difficult and unwanted ones, the Agency learned it well. Throughout the development process Yerba Buena has illustrated that challengers can serve as educators, teaching how to incorporate conflict into the process and how to listen to divergent points of view. Taking this lesson to heart and including all voices – including local residents – can be difficult and frustrating, but it produces more vibrant and ultimately more viable results. This is particularly true if the forums created to enable people to talk to each other about a specific issues – say, for example, housing – are institutionalized so that discussion and negotiation can continue after the initial response has been formulated.

- *Process, program, and management should reflect a commitment to a place and be inclusive of the human communities and relationships that constitute it.*

Yerba Buena's central open Garden announces one of the most important values embodied in the design process: this is a public space, open to all residents and visitors. The Agency came to recognize that valuing a place meant recognizing how different constituencies value it, and that commitment to a place means a commitment to the communities who thus value it. A design process built on such a commitment meant involving local community voices, making use and programming of facilities inclusive and welcoming, creating an open and accessible design, and fostering an ongoing dialogue among residents, institutions, and businesses.

FOR FURTHER INFORMATION

Cheryl Parker, "Making a 21st century neighborhood," *Places* (vol. 10 #1, 1995, pp. 36-45). *Suggests that the South of Market Area (SOMA) can be a prototype of the desirable "pocket community." Pocket communities are a neighborhood-like miniature residential infill with mixed living/working buildings in mixed-used areas. Such developments, Parker proposes, offer an alternative to the large-scale commercial and residential development typical of post-industrial urban evolution.*

Ibid. "A story of change: Re-making San Francisco," (Masters Thesis, UC Berkeley, 1993). *The more expansive piece from which "Making a 21st century neighborhood" was compiled.*

Chester Hartman, *Yerba Buena: Land Grab and Community Resistance in San Francisco.* (San Francisco: Glide Publications, 1974). *Written during the days of the Redevelopment Authority's first effort at Yerba Buena, Harman reveals just how bad the "bad old days" were. His chilling examples and powerful narrative depict a city office brought down by its own arrogance. Essential reading for understanding (a) why TODCO came into being, and (b) just how radical the Redevelopment Authority's re-orientation has been since TODCO put an end to Yerba Buena's first era.*

John Elberling, "An urban layer cake," *SF Bay Guardian,* (November 17, 1993, pp. 14-15). *Elberling, a TODCO officer, explains that "[w]hat has been built and what is yet to come was planned much more by local politics than by the architects and planners of official record." His newspaper article goes through each Mayor and respective "cake layer."*

Sally B. Woodbridge, "When good urban plans go awry (Yerba Buena Gardens, San Francisco)," *Progressive Architecture,* (vol. 76, Nov. 1995, pp. 60-67). *Despite the efforts of many noted architects and landscape architects, Woodbridge argues, the area still looks cobbled together, in part because of the almost 30 years of false starts for the development.*

Clifford A. Pearson, "Metreon, San Francisco, California: What's a shopping and entertainment center doing in an arts complex? Keeping the place busy around the clock," *Architectural Record* (vol. 10, 1999, pp.154-160).

Related Rudy Bruner Award Winners

(For full bibliographic cites, please see Introduction)

Portland's 1972 Downtown Plan (1989 cycle). A successful comprehensive planning process for downtown development that has engendered diverse uses (a "24-hour place"), a pedestrian focus, historic buildings, public open spaces, and improved air quality.

Lowerton, Saint Paul, Minnesota (1995 cycle). The redevelopment of a historic district near the downtown by a small private non-profit organization that has created a lively, mixed income and mixed use area, including retail, office, and low-mod and market rate housing.

Center in the Square, Roanoke, Virginia (1997 cycle). A downtown cultural center that brings together a group of cultural entities in a rent-free space. Created a new cultural and educational destination in Roanoke, and has sparked the revitalization of downtown.

Contacts

San Francisco Redevelopment Agency
770 Golden Gate Ave, San Francisco, CA 94102
Helen Sause, Deputy Director
415-749-2506, helen_sause@ci.sf.ca.us
William Carney, Project Director
415-749-2412, bill_carney@ci.sf.ca.us
Catherine Pickering, Development Specialist
415-749-2519, cathy_pickering@ci.sf.ca.us

Yerba Buena Alliance
Anita Hill, Executive Director,
415-541-0312, yballiance@yerbabuena.org

Yerba Buena Consortium
John Elberling, Chair,
415-896-1882, jetodco@todco.org

Yerba Buena Center for the Arts
John Killacky, Executive Director,
415-978-2710 x101, jkillacky@yerbabuenaarts.org

Zeum
David Dial, Executive Director,
415-284-7114,ddial@zeum.org

KTB Realty Partners, Inc.
Mary McCue, Gardens General Manager,
415-247-6500, mary.mccue@ktbrealty.com

Metreon
Kari Novatney, General Manager,
415-369-6005, Kari@sre.sony.com

Moscone Center
Julie Burford, Assistant General Manager,
415-284-7119, jburford@moscone.com

RUDY BRUNER AWARD
FOR URBAN EXCELLENCE

BRUNER FOUNDATION
130 Prospect Street
Cambridge, MA 02139
PH: 617.492.8404
FX: 617.876.4002

www.brunerfoundation.org

1999 Rudy Bruner Award

SILVER
medal winner

PORTLAND PUBLIC MARKET

Portland, Maine

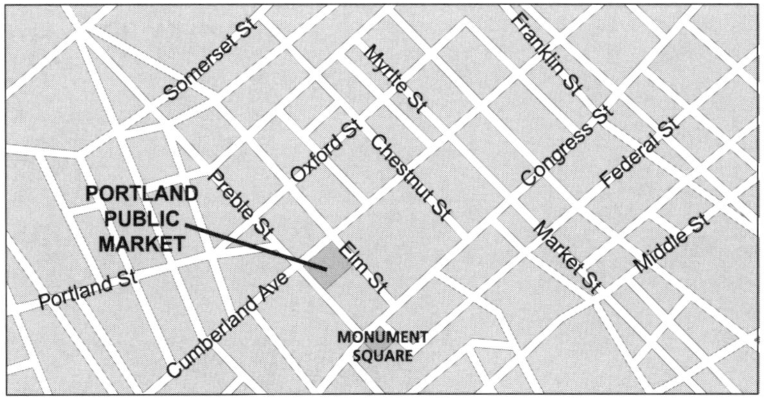
Somerset St
Myrtle St
Franklin St
Oxford St
Chestnut St
Congress St
Federal St
PORTLAND PUBLIC MARKET
Preble St
Elm St
Market St
Middle St
Portland St
Cumberland Ave
MONUMENT SQUARE

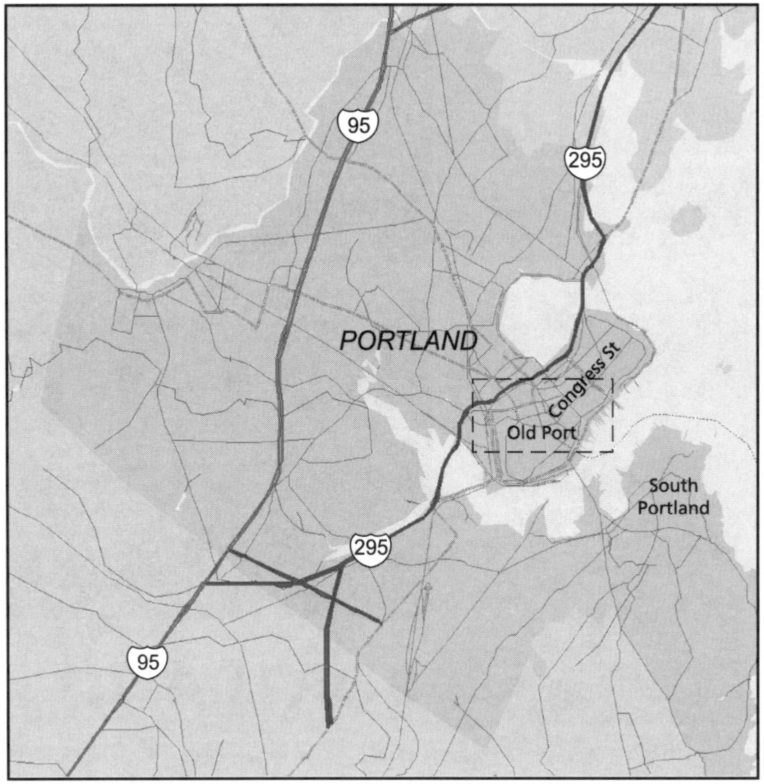
95
295
PORTLAND
Congress St
Old Port
South Portland
295
95

PORTLAND PUBLIC MARKET AT A GLANCE

WHO MADE THE SUBMISSION?

- Portland Public Market; Theodore Spitzer, Director.

WHAT IS THE PORTLAND PUBLIC MARKET?

- A newly constructed indoor fresh food market that houses up to 28 permanent vendors selling Maine-based agricultural products, fresh food and flowers, and eight day tables for small farmers and food producers.

- A commercial development intended to spur renewal in a neglected "marginal" area of downtown Portland while offering a venue for Maine's struggling small family farmers.

- A four-season indoor market that complements Portland's existing outdoor farmer's market.

- A new model for philanthropic intervention in downtown revitalization.

- A well-designed new building constructed by Maine laborers with Maine products.

CHRONOLOGY

LATE 1970's-1980's
Downtown Maine begins an economic decline; building vacancies increase.

1989
Philanthropist Elizabeth Noyce starts the successful Maine Bank & Trust after other local banks fail.

1990
City Council creates Downtown Portland Corporation, a low interest-lending source to stimulate investment in the downtown.

1990
Elizabeth Noyce's October Corporation buys 3 office buildings downtown, one to house Maine Bank & Trust and to provide an anchor on Congress Street.

1993-1994
Elizabeth Noyce entices L.L. Bean and Olympia Sports to downtown Portland by subsidizing their buildout.

1995
Portland Public Market conceived; Theodore Spitzer undertakes feasability analysis and conceptual plan.

1996
Spitzer hired as Project Director and Hugh Boyd hired as architect.

1997
Groundbreaking.

OCT. 6, 1998
Market opens to the public.

KEY PARTICIPANTS

Individuals who were interviewed are marked with an asterisk [*]

Portland Public Market

*Theodore Spitzer, Director
*Elizabeth Finegan, Marketing Director

City of Portland

*George Campbell, City Councilor, former Mayor of Portland
*Kathleen Brown, Director, Economic Development, City of Portland
*Barbara Hagar, Director, Portland's Downtown District

Funding

Elizabeth Noyce, philanthropist (deceased)
*Owen Wells, President, Libra Foundation and President, October Corporation

Design & Construction

*Hugh Boyd, AIA, Principal, Hugh A. Boyd Architecture
*John Orcutt, AIA, Principal, Orcutt Associates
*John Blanchard, President, HE Callahan Construction Co.

Community Consultants

*Dennis Pratt, Alpha One Access Consultants
*Mark Swann, Executive Director, Preble Street Resource Center
*Dan O'Leary, Director, Portland Museum of Art
*Joe Boulos, President, The Boulos Company

1989 Elizabeth Noyce founds Maine Bank & Trust
1990 October Corp. buys key downtown bldgs.
1995 Idea for public market conceived
1996 Favorable market analysis completed
1999 Portland Public Market opens

PROJECT DESCRIPTION

HISTORY

The Portland Public Market is the crown jewel of local philanthropist Elizabeth Noyce's efforts to reverse the decline of downtown Portland. Once thriving, the city center was seriously weakened when a major suburban mall located nearby in 1970, and was further devastated by the recession of the late 1980s. Together these factors left downtown Portland largely abandoned by both retail and office use. Merchants estimated vacancy rates in commercial buildings as high as 90% during the early 1990s, and empty retail locations were a common sight. At the height of the recession the two major banks in Portland failed, leaving the city without a banking institution of any significance – the proverbial "nail in the coffin" for a dying downtown.

Elizabeth Noyce moved to Maine after her 1975 divorce from Robert Noyce, inventor of the Intel computer chip; with her came a large settlement of Intel stock that she used to establish the philanthropic Libra Foundation. She observed the abandonment of downtown Portland with dismay, and in 1990 she resolved to act. Having previously used an out-of-state bank, Mrs. Noyce decided that year to start her own bank in Portland and use it as a catalyst for the redevelopment of the downtown. As the Maine Bank & Trust grew, Mrs. Noyce bought a building just off Monument Square, the neglected historic center of Portland, as well as two other office buildings nearby as part of the same transaction. These buildings had high vacancy rates, required significant investment, and lacked adequate parking. Noyce brought the buildings up to standards and purchased a 650-space garage on a lot nearby.

These early steps illustrated what would become Mrs. Noyce's and Libra's trademark strategy: "economic philanthropy." Essentially, it meant negotiating to bring in businesses just as a private developer, landlord, or in some cases a city ordinarily would, except that – being philanthropic – it would have lower expectations of financial returns and would be willing to assume higher risk than conventional developers. Thus, after witnessing the departure of

Congress Street at Monument Square. The two office buildings on the upper right, purchased by Elizabeth Noyce's foundation, frame the entrance to Preble Street and the Portland Public Market.

Portland's last department store in 1992 and the subsequent collapse of retail on Congress Street, Mrs. Noyce purchased a vacant building on Congress and brought in L.L. Bean as a tenant. She offered the skeptical catalogue company a minimal-risk, short-term lease and money for fit-out if it would open its first ever retail outlet in a central city. The same kind of enticements convinced Olympia Sports, another Maine-based company, to open shop next to L.L. Bean the following year. The technique, City Councilor and former Mayor George Campbell noted, resembles Urban Development Action Grants (a federal program that funneled development money into the private sector).

Owen Wells, who would become President of the Libra Foundation after Noyce's death, conceived of the Portland Public Market while on vacation in 1995. Wells had been head of the Portland Museum of Art in the 1980s and had met Noyce in the course of raising money to expand the museum. He became a confidante and trusted advisor to Noyce, playing important roles in key decisions such as opening the downtown bank. In 1995 Wells visited both Pike Place Market in Seattle and the Granville Island Public Market in Vancouver. Excited by the energy and impact of these places, he suggested to Noyce that they create a public market in Portland as part of their continuing effort to revitalize the downtown.

Noyce agreed that the idea was intriguing, and Wells contacted Theodore Spitzer, co-author of a book of case studies called *Public Markets and Community Revitalization* (1995) and a veteran of public market developments in New York City, Columbus, Philadelphia, and New Orleans. Spitzer agreed to undertake a feasibility study. The study proved favorable, identifying a two-century tradition of public markets in Portland and suggesting that the region around the small city held enough potential customers to support a marquee market. The study bore the trademarks of Spitzer's community development approach to public markets: it highlighted how the market would provide a much needed boost for downtown businesses as well as for Maine farmers, and how it could offer a public space to bring together Portland's diverse population. While the Market could not carry a debt load, each of the proposed tenants should be able to operate profitably and pay adequate rents to cover operating costs following a reasonable start-up period. According to Spitzer, a few days after he sent in the feasibility report he received a phone call from Wells: "Let's build it, and by the way, will you manage the project for us?"

Although Elizabeth Noyce died unexpectedly in the fall of that same year, the project continued to move forward under the guidance of Wells and Spitzer. Spitzer founded Market Ventures, Inc., which managed the development and now provides day-to-day management of the Market under contract with the August Corporation. Hugh Boyd was hired as architect in 1996, and two years later in October the market opened to surprisingly widespread media notice (articles appeared in *The Boston Globe* and *The New York Times*, for example).

VISION

The most obvious vision inspiring the Portland Public Market is Noyce's innovative strategy of philanthropy in the service of economic development. Ordinarily, the Selection Committee observed, community foundations do not enter the economic development arena, staying instead in their traditional territory of "arm's length" support for providers of economic, social, and cultural programs. Through various interventions into downtown Portland, Mrs. Noyce and the Libra Foundation have offered a vision of how philanthropy can redefine its role in the community and assume a broader position of responsibility and impact. The Market exemplifies this philosophy. Conceived from the beginning as a philanthropic project, it was designed to revive a dying downtown by solidifying Portland's "spine" and connecting the tourist-oriented "Old Port" area to the developing arts district. The Committee was impressed by the skill of the intervention; although quite small – as little as one-fourth the size of a large "big box" supermarket – it is obviously "a big deal in a little city."

As people enter from the sky bridge at the mezzanine level they are afforded an overview of the Market floor.

The Market has also been fundamentally informed by the social justice agenda that Spitzer has continually brought to his work. Thus, the Market is not just any retail development designed to bring cash into the downtown; rather, it is a public space that strengthens communities within Portland, supports neighboring social service agencies, and affirms or forges bonds between the City of Portland and Maine farmers. The stalls offer a retail venue for the state's hard-hit small farmers and independent food producers, and the educational bent of the Market's operations encourages learning about where food comes from and dramatizes the value of buying local products. This "retail edutainment," the Committee felt, was an innovative and quite successful way for the Market to move beyond purely commercial activities without embracing touristy clichés or faux traditions. It added value to the consumer experience, while at the same time teaching shoppers about (and thus strengthening) their already existing relationships to their state's farmers.

Spitzer also envisioned the Market as connected to its urban surroundings in concrete ways. The clearest example of this vision is the story of the Preble Street Resource Center, one of the many social service providers in the Bayside neighborhood around the

Market. When Spitzer first contacted the organization, Preble's Executive Director Mark Swann recalls, he assumed that Spitzer wanted to discuss "how to keep Preble Street clients away from the Market." Instead, Swann was pleased to learn that Spitzer wanted to explore how they "could work together and involve Preble Street in a constructive way." Spitzer's commitment to this goal was proven shortly thereafter, when Stone Soup, Preble Street's first business venture, secured a vendor stall in the Market (see "Stone Soup Foods" in "Vendors" below). The Selection Committee noted that this community outreach is only one of several visible examples of the project's social agenda.

Both Noyce and Spitzer conceived of the Market as an authentic part of the City of Portland. One Selection Committee member agreed that this is no "franchise excuse for a city," but a Market that genuinely reflects the distinctive people who live and work in Portland and in Maine. In the words of another Committee member, the project has "avoided the scented-candle effect" through careful choice of vendors (see "Vendors" below), targeted lease structures (see "Financing" below), the consistent values of management, and Libra Foundation's distant but significant oversight.

ORGANIZATION AND LEADERSHIP

The Market staff is organized in a fairly simple way: Spitzer serves as Director working with seven employees divided into two teams. The professional office-based team answers directly to Spitzer, and consists of marketing director Elizabeth Finegan, an office manager, and a vendor coordinator. The second team, the porter staff, includes four people, one of whom is quasi-supervisory. Overall, the staff are well prepared for their jobs; in particular, Finegan comes to the project with marketing experience from public markets in Philadelphia and Baltimore.

Ted Spitzer

Although Elizabeth Noyce, Owen Wells, and the Libra Foundation were the prime movers in this project, Ted Spitzer has provided the operational leadership. Before being hired by Libra, Spitzer had already been involved in the renaissance of public markets across the nation. He had helped develop several markets, and with Hilary Baum ran the Public Markets Partners, founded in 1991. The Partners organization provides technical assistance on the development and operation of markets nationwide, has operated open-air markets in low-income communities in New York City, and promotes awareness of markets through educational materials.

Spitzer's deep experience helped him in the early, delicate task of assuaging the doubts of farmers at the existing outdoor farmers' market at Monument Square. As Spitzer's feasibility report remarked, these farmers needed "to be persuaded of the advantages of a public market – they are not seeking to escape from a bad situation." Some farmers were worried that the new market would displace them; others recognized the need to expand their customer base and retail space, but were unsure about their ability to start a higher-overhead operation. Spitzer worked with them to minimize product competition. Since the outdoor market sells produce and flowers, the indoor market emphasizes meats, fish, and other foods. Spitzer also marshaled positive evidence from his experiences with other public markets to persuade the farmers that additional choice of products would attract more customers and that these additional customers would benefit everyone in the area.

Farmers were not the only ones who needed convincing. According to Joe Boulos, whose real estate firm manages all of the other properties owned by Libra Foundation, conventional wisdom predicted failure for all of Noyce's projects, including the bank and the market. People had basically given up on the east side of Congress Street, he explains; the prevailing view was that "no one in their right mind" would put nearly $10 million into a market there. Even the downtown Business Improvement District expressed little confidence. But for Noyce, who was content to break even, this skepticism only reinforced the need for a public investment or private philanthropy – development would obviously not happen through conventional channels. Determinedly optimistic, she and Spitzer reamined committed to downtown Portland.

Indeed, Spitzer has repeatedly demonstrated his commitment both to the success of the Market and to his vision for what the Market can mean for Portland. Spitzer and his whole staff, for example, have their salaries tied to the Market's bottom line. He has also worked assiduously to prevent, or at least limit, the "gentrification" of the Market. This goal is reflected in the lease structures, which favor farmers and food producers selling fresh products over vendors selling others' products or prepared foods. Crafts and general merchandise are not permitted. In general, the vendor mix has been carefully chosen to create a "real" market, useful for Maine residents first and foremost, and of interest to tourists because of its authenticity. Additionally, Spitzer made it clear that the Market should provide shopping opportunities and community space for local residents, including the 800 elderly and low-income residents of the surrounding Bayside neighborhood. The Preble Street story (see "Vendors" below) speaks to this commitment.

Spitzer's commitment to the project and to the project's beneficial role in the community has been an important part of the Market's success to date. While the Market is by no means a democracy – Spitzer hears suggestions, but makes the decisions himself – it has benefited greatly from Spitzer's willingness to seek out and then listen to the input of others. A case in point is the Market's effort to accommodate the disabled. This was an especially difficult goal given the physical characteristics of the site, a steep slope with different floor elevations at every corner of the building. Spitzer and Boyd sought out Alpha One, a local consultant on disability issues, and worked with them from the start to create a fully accessible public space. Although the access solution involved sloping floors throughout the Market, and additional costs were high, the Market remained committed to this goal.

The Selection Committee initially wondered whether Spitzer's leadership might be a little *too* good – in other words, might the project depend entirely on his personal nurturance and commitment to authenticity and community outreach? Ultimately, however, the

Committee came to the conclusion that the Market has established organizational dynamics that should survive Spitzer's departure, in particular the lease structure and the tying of management salaries to the bottom line (see "Finance" below) as well as Libra Foundation's continuing interest in the project.

DESIGN

Urban Context

At 65,000 residents, Portland is the largest city in Maine and the only major city in the southern portion of the state. The greater Portland area is home to about 217,000 people, who enjoy a surprisingly low local unemployment rate of 2%. Just beyond the city edges, however, Maine farmers, like others across the country, are struggling to keep their land in active agricultural use. Farmland, especially land close to Portland or other Maine cities, can be more profitably sold for development.

There are three main foci in downtown Portland. First, Portland's "cultural corridor" extends along Congress Street from the Portland Museum of Art (which includes an outstanding collection of paintings by Maine artists such as Winslow Homer and Andrew Wyeth, many of which were donated by Noyce) to the Maine College of Art (located in the former Porteous Department Store), the Merrill Hall performance Center, the Children's Museum, and Portland Stage Company. The synergy of these institutions, located in close proximity to each other and encompassing Monument Square, the titular "center" of the City, make a convenient destination for locals and visitors arriving in Portland. That connection is strengthened by steadily growing economic activity along Congress Street, including the Maine Bank & Trust established by Mrs. Noyce, the L.L. Bean and Olympia Sports retail stores, and more recent independent additions such as a Starbucks Coffee in a historic building near the Art Museum.

The second downtown focus is the Old Port, a series of shops and restaurants located in historic buildings along the waterfront. The Old Port has long been a major attraction for visitors to the

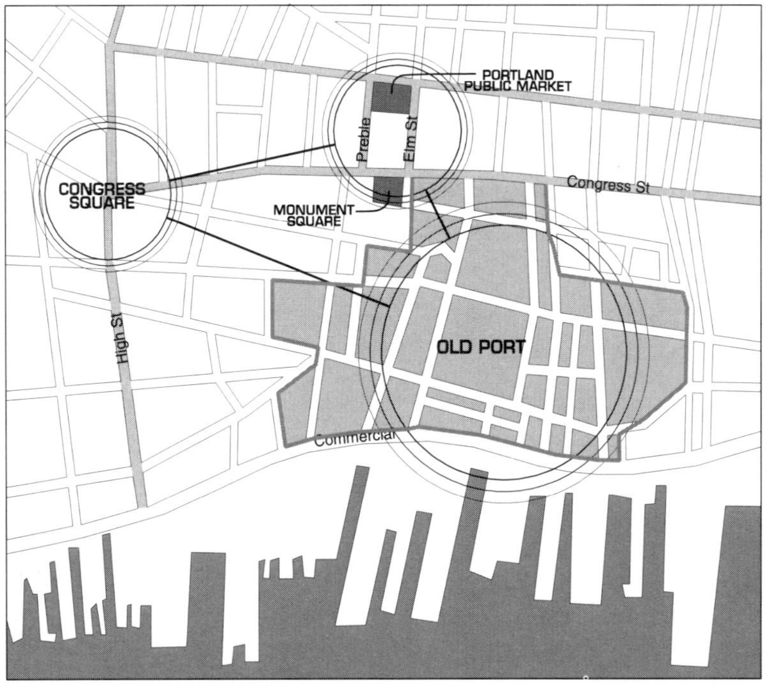

Urban context of downtown Portland

Portland area. Its narrow cobbled streets and historic brick buildings make it an attractive destination for visitors arriving either by car or by boat. It begins several blocks from Monument Square, on the opposite side of Congress Street from the Market. The shops are pedestrian-friendly, and visitors can easily find their way to the nearby cultural facilities.

The Bayside neighborhood, where the Portland Public Market is located, has historically been the "poor neighbor" to the cultural corridor and Old Port. With Congress Street as a divider, the neighborhood is home to 75 nonprofit agencies providing services to the poor and elderly, as well as a number of government agencies and small businesses. It was considered an unsafe neighborhood, offering little to either visitors or residents. Construction of Noyce's parking garage was the first significant development in the area in many years, followed by the development of the Public Market.

Libra Foundation expanded its investments in Bayside by purchasing six additional acres in 1998 on the opposite side of the parking garage from the Market. The Foundation has offered to donate part of the land for the construction of a new sports and entertainment complex to replace the city's aging civic center. Many attribute the potential viability of this plan to the presence of the Market, and the way in which it has made Bayside an attractive and integral part of the downtown.

Architecture

The Market Building

From the start Elizabeth Noyce wanted the Portland Public Market to be a welcoming place, and a major gathering place for all segments of the Portland community. In addition, she felt the design and construction of the Market should benefit Maine residents and workers. She placed a priority on using materials and contractors from Maine, creating numerous jobs in the construction phase and benefiting the Maine craftsmen who produced most of the building materials. The Market was to be a stimulus for revitalizing Bayside and an incubator for small businesses.

The Market is geared to many types of users.

To realize this vision, Spitzer sought the services of Hugh Boyd, a New Jersey architect who specializes in public market architecture and the design of retail food businesses, and Orcutt Associates, a Portland area firm that understood local conditions. Boyd's involvement began with the 1995 feasibility study, and he clearly understood both Spitzer's approach and Noyce's intent. For him, part of this meant "a great deal of emphasis . . . on using indigenous materials in keeping with Portland's historic downtown buildings." The 37,000 square-foot market utilizes a palette of locally produced brick, white pine decking, and Deer Isle granite, which is also found on the building exterior, plaza, and sidewalks. The wood ceiling and intricate geometry of Douglas Fir timber trusses and rafters, sitting atop concrete columns, are intended to add warmth to the building and animate the high ceiling space, relating to a historic barn vernacular. Although the wood itself had to be imported from Oregon due to the lengths of trusses required, Maine timber framers, who pride themselves on their art, put the framing together. They insisted on pegged connections rather than nails throughout the timber elements. The Timber Framers' Guild also participated. When more skilled help was needed, as many as 30 framers worked together at critical moments during the erection of the roof trusses. This community-wide craft effort is consistent with the barn raising models of construction from earlier centuries in Maine.

The building is located on an L-shaped site that slopes in two directions, presenting a considerable design challenge, particularly with respect to accessibility. Major doorways at three locations welcome visitors and customers approaching from different directions, and full-height glass windows on the exterior walls are intended to create maximum transparency between the interior and exterior. To accommodate the considerable slopes of the two L-segments and to keep them both fully accessible, the floor of the Market itself is subtly sloped, although the grade change is barely perceptible as one traverses the spaces. The two-story height of the market space creates an open, airy feeling, and allows balcony seating along two walls, giving seated customers a good view of the market activity below.

Hanson Brothers seafood display

The most significant design challenge was to provide space and infrastructure for the extensive mechanical and electrical needs of the food vendors, including bread ovens, refrigeration, showcases, and illuminated displays. Boyd personally designed every tenant space, balancing the need to promote individual expression with efficient layouts and a high level of quality throughout. Individual vendor stalls line two sloping internal aisles on each of the building's two wings. This configuration creates four islands that contain vendors selling produce, desserts, prepared food, cheeses, coffee, and flowers. Vendors with heavy cooking and refrigeration requirements, such as bakers, butchers, and seafood businesses, are located along the rear wall of the building, where their equipment won't block sight lines and where it can be easily vented to a lower roof. Vendors with lighter back-of-house requirements, such as a dairy, wine shop, and specialty food store, occupy the spaces on the outer glass wall.

The building is intended to serve as a backdrop, with the major drama coming from the food presentation itself. Explains Boyd, "the arrangement and location of the individual vendors were carefully choreographed to accentuate the vendors' visual strengths, theatrical opportunities for displays, and exposed preparation areas." Food is displayed under halogen lighting on carefully designed refrigeration cases and display tables. Walking through the Market the sights and smells of food displayed or being prepared are compelling. The food and vendors are accessible, eager to tell the stories of their products. Ample seating contributes to the inviting character. A central fireplace, made from Deer Isle granite,

The douglas fir timber trusses and rafters sit on concrete columns, and were placed by the Timber Framers Guild.

One of the design challenges was to address the grade changes in a seamless and fully accessible fashion.

enhances the quality of the Market as a community-gathering place. Built-in granite benches surrounding the fireplace make the Market feel welcoming, particularly in a city with a long winter, harsh climate, and many gray overcast days.

Unfortunately, even though the Market is air-conditioned, the extensive use of glass results in excessive solar heating. Mechanized, retractable translucent shades, which can be lowered as needed, were installed several months after opening following problems with sunshine spoiling some foods and rising utility bills. Several compromises were also made in the design process. The architect wanted the building to have a copper roof, but feels that the less expensive metal selected works from a design perspective. Ironically, the price of copper has since decreased, making it almost as cost-effective as the material actually used.

Overall, the Selection Committee recognized the high quality of the Market's architecture – one member made a pointed comparison to typical mall design – but did not feel that it was, on its own, as meritorious as the social programming that had gone into the building's function.

From the Street

On the exterior of the building, specially designed metal canopies shelter the passerby from inclement weather and offer space for future outdoor vending. The transparency of the Market lends a glowing, warm light to the street at night, creating a kind of beacon in the neighborhood. The transparency is somewhat diminished, however, by the tall display spaces behind the counters of the stalls, which obscure large areas of window. Vendors are working to develop attractive window displays behind these cases, but at the time of our visit many of these displays had not yet been installed.

The City of Portland paid for sidewalk and street improvements around the Market, and the wide brick sidewalks, attractive street lights, and granite curbing reinforce the building's design vocabulary while extending its welcome to the street. Across Preble Street there are a variety of businesses including a wine shop, a pub, and several offices, which benefit from the patronage of the market, while offering slightly different products. This extension of commercial activity reinforces the attraction and safety of the street.

Street entrance at the intersection of Preble Street and Cumberland Ave.

Directly across from both the east and north sides of the Market are two parking garages. One is owned by the city, and is attractively designed in brick, complementing to some extent the design of the Market. The second, built by Mrs. Noyce, is less attractive in its design, but is connected by a skybridge to the Market. Both parking garages pose problems at the pedestrian level, inasmuch as they offer no opportunity for additional retail activity on the street. However, the latter garage does provide free parking and sheltered access for Market customers as well as one retail space for the dry cleaner relocated from the Market site.

The skybridge connecting the garage to the Market is the first such pedestrian bridge over a public right-of-way to be built in Maine. As such, State permit agencies had difficulty understanding it, and initially required it to be structured to accommodate motor vehicles. Eventually these design issues were settled, and a pedestrian-oriented design was developed. The development team initially opposed it, because one of their major goals was to activate the street with pedestrians. However, the skybridge, which the Foundation strongly supported, has proven to be an asset not only for the protection it provides from frequently inhospitable weather, but as an attraction in and of itself, offering a unique vantage point to view the city. It is designed to be consistent with the Market, with floor-to-ceiling glass, and a transparent quality echoing that of the Market itself.

The Selection Committee noted that the Market's designers had "read their audience well." By providing a well-lit market building and a skybridge entryway the building was welcoming to people who might be wary of shopping in a formerly run-down and perhaps even dangerous section of Portland.

VENDORS

The mix of vendors has been carefully, almost painstakingly selected by the management team to support the goal of an authentic market that helps sustain Maine's endangered agricultural economy. Organic small farms are the only expanding segment of the Maine agricultural sector, and the Market promises to be a significant outlet for those producers. At the same time the Market provides economic opportunity, and in some cases support, for small start-up businesses that might not otherwise exist. In a larger sense, Spitzer hopes to assist in mainstreaming some of the goods produced by Maine farmers. As he explained, "We'll know we have been successful when these kinds of products are carried at Shop 'n' Save."

By the same token, there was a deliberate effort to avoid creating a market of prepared fast foods catering only to lunch-time diners. In addition to the producer-friendly lease structure, each vendor's offerings are strictly regulated to avoid this sort of dynamic. There is a shared commitment among vendors and management to take the time to develop a broad-based clientele of regular, consistent, repeat customers. The vendor mix therefore includes seafood, dairy, meat, poultry, baked goods, specialty foods, and changing products on the day tables (rented out on a short-term basis). The broader selection offers visitors looking for snacks and meals a variety of products to eat on the premises, and a mix of food for home preparation. The Selection Committee affirmed management's

The floor plan for the Market allows users to see several vendors at a glance.

choices, finding the resulting vendor mix to be "creative, purposeful, and principled."

Spitzer's previous experience had taught him that competition would increase the quality of the market and would ultimately benefit the vendors. Many vendors admitted that they were concerned about moving into a setting where others would be selling similar products in close proximity to their own. All have become convinced, however, that having "internal competition" of that kind draws more customers, and provides stimulus for keeping their own businesses and products fresh and competitive. Management also put forth a conscious effort to include both experienced retailers and start-ups, with the hope that the retailing neophytes could learn quickly by observing their more experienced counterparts.

The feeling of camaraderie and cooperation among the vendors was palpable. As they put it, they all either fail or succeed together. Most are careful not to encroach on each other's product territory, and refer customers to each other for certain items. They also shop liberally from each other's wares. All reported that they are generally happy with management. Monthly vendor meetings are focused on miscellaneous small issues, but no major disagreements with management seem to have emerged to date.

Vendors have attained a surprising degree of success in reaching their economic goals, sooner in many cases than projected. The Market opened on October of 1998, with many vendors frustrated by having missed the summer season due to construction delays, which caused some to lose food they had prepared for the postponed opening. Overall they enjoyed tremendous success during the holiday season, have experienced a slowdown in the winter months, but are experiencing increasing sales as the weather softens. Many have exceeded their second- and third-year projections already. All vendors were extremely hopeful about the summer season, with many of them increasing production. In general terms the relatively high square-foot lease cost (see Finances below) is compensated by the synergy among vendors and the customer volume brought in by the Market's "one-stop shopping" appeal.

Vendor Stories

Borealis Breads

Borealis Breads, run by Jim Amaral, is one of the more visible and sizable vendors in the Market. Bread is baked on the premises, with "bread theater" visible to customers. Amaral says that on a slow day he has approximately 300 transactions, but at the holiday rush he reached 900-1,100 transactions per day. Borealis begins mixing, kneading, and rising the dough late at night so that the breads come out of the oven when the doors of the Market first open, permeating the building with the smell of fresh baking. "We're open at 7 am to provide customers with a warm breakfast roll on their way to work," Amaral says.

Owing to the success of his Market stall (projecting $600,000 in sales this year) and his interest in supporting Maine farmers, Amaral has contracted with several farmers in hard-pressed Aroostook

County to plant 40 acres of organic wheat for Borealis' three bakeries. This is an historically significant step, as Aroostook was once the bread basket of the United States and has been losing farmland at a rapid rate. The success of this pilot wheat-growing program in its first year has led Amaral to greatly expand the effort. Part of his larger project is to explore the potential of revitalizing Maine's once-thriving agricultural economy through specialty foods like organic wheat, grown using high-yield farming techniques. Wheat production is anticipated to be a ton an acre, or 70,000 pounds of wheat a year; excess crop not used by Borealis will be sold on the open market.

Smiling Hill Farm

Smiling Hill Farm has been in the Knight family for two centuries. Recently, because of its close proximity to Portland, development pressures have made it difficult to maintain the farm. Smiling Hill, in fact, is the only dairy farm left among hundreds that once operated in the vicinity. To keep the farm in operation, the family has turned to "agri-tourism," offering an extensive petting farm and open barns to encourage families to come to the farm and watch the milk being made; opening an ice cream and sandwich shop; providing space for cross-country skiing; and introducing other revenue-producing efforts like a lumber yard, an on-farm

Bread baking at Borealis Breads as part of the food theater in the public market.

Market vendors take care in the maintenance of the Market and in the artful display of their products.

facility to bottle milk in glass containers, and an ice-creamery. Like Borealis and other vendors engaging in "food theater," the Knight family believes that people want to be connected to the process of food creation and are interested in seeing and knowing where their food comes from.

In the Market, Smiling Hill provides a wide array of dairy products with its own signature flavor and richness. Although it has not yet achieved the profitability they projected, they are committed to remaining at the Market. They hope that the summer season will help them attain their market projections.

Valley View Orchards Farm

One of the big success stories of the Market is Valley View Orchards Farm. Originally apple farmers, the owners turned to pie baking as apple prices plummeted in response to increasingly cheap imports from South America. The family began with small local pie distribution, but then expanded as the pie business proved more successful than they had anticipated. In the first year they made 5,000 pies; in the second year, 15,000 pies; today they make up to 100,000 pies per year, which they sell wholesale and retail.

Valley View was interested in the Portland Public Market from the beginning. Business at the Portland Public Market has far exceeded their expectations, particularly during the holiday season – they were completely sold out for both Thanksgiving and Christmas. They stated that they could easily use double the space they have in the Market. During their first six months of operation, Valley View has exceeded its first-year goal of $8-$10,000 profit by 25%.

Java Joe's

Java Joe's sells gourmet coffees by the pound, brewed coffee, and espresso drinks, plus teas and chocolates. Joanna and Cory Morrissey, who founded their first coffee shop in the Old Port, have exceeded their three-year projections in the first six months of operation, averaging about 300 transactions a day at about $2.00 per transaction.

Stone Soup Foods

The Selection Committee felt that Stone Soup was one of the Market's most interesting and important stories. Mark Swann, director of Preble Street Resource Center, has been involved in providing social services in the Bayside neighborhood for 25 years. When Spitzer first contacted Swann, Preble Street was running a soup kitchen serving 350 meals a day. Swann was pleasantly surprised by Spitzer's commitment to incorporate the Center into the Market in a way that would provide job opportunities and would support the Center's mission. The two soon agreed that the agency should expand their meals program with a retail soup shop in the Market. Stone Soup, which sells quality soups prepared by professional chefs, also serves as a training program for Preble Street clientele in the retail business. Job training includes a 12-week program offered through the Center, with two of those weeks on site at Stone Soup. Swann also noted that other vendors contribute to his enterprise by giving them leftover food, bones, and other items that can be used in soups. In exchange, Stone Soup advertises those vendors and their ingredients.

As of April, 1999, Stone Soup is above its best case projections by 30%, and is profiting at a rate of about $1,000/month net. From this new base of operations they hope to add office catering, improve the retail component of their stand, and offer dried soup mixes. In addition, being in the Market has been great publicity for Preble Street. Annual giving has increased by 75%, attributable, Swann thinks, to their increased visibility. On opening day, for example, an impressed benefactor came to the Stone Soup counter and wrote Swann a $20,000 check for the Center.

Hanson Brothers seafood features local and exotic fish.

Hanson Brothers Seafood

Local entrepreneur Brian Hanson is the owner of this seafood business, and also served as tenant coordinator during the construction process. He recruited Walter Compare from Pike Place Market to run his business in the Market, and has created a combination retail seafood stall and oyster bar cafe. Hanson Brothers has exceeded its projections for this point in the year, and hopes to double its sales this summer. Their stall and adjacent restaurant are highly visible, and shoppers are also attracted to their sophisticated displays, which feature a wide variety of dramatically presented fish and seafood.

Day Tables

The day tables, rented on a short-term basis, house both start-up vendors and past and present outdoor farmer's market vendors. Although day table vendors concede that they do not enjoy the community and amenities of the long-term vendors – the marketing effort puts most of its emphasis on identifying and promoting long-term vendors – they do appreciate the invariably good table locations, the niceties of indoor life, and the helpfulness of other Market tenants. These tables allow a greater flexibility to the Market product mix, particularly in regard to seasonal products. Like the longer-term stalls, the lease structure for the day tables favors farmers and food producers over retailers and fast food vendors. In the first six months of the Market's operation, over 60 individuals took advantage of the day table program. Some, such as two goat cheese producers, requested and were granted the same space for one day per week over a nine-month period.

Day tables are an important part of the life of the Market.

PROGRAMS

The Market publicizes a wide variety of programs through its newsletter *The Crier*, its website, and more conventional advertising and public service announcements. Offered in the upstairs kitchen facility are cooking classes and the Cooking Club (nine meetings for $25), which features weekly discussions and cooking demonstrations on a different topic ranging from wine and cheese pairings to presentations on ethnic cuisine. The fall *Crier* advertised after-school children's programs, such as teaching kids how to make bread wreaths and fruit pizza. Local chefs and restaurateurs join vendors in providing instruction. The newsletter also announces availability of day stalls, updates the foods being offered and featured according to the season, provides a calendar of topics and

Cooking classes are educational and help promote market vendors.

chefs for upcoming cooking classes, offers brief biographies of guest chefs, and publicizes the availability of the Market for private and public events.

Beyond food-related events, the program agenda includes a Sunday music series in the Market and a "News from the Market" section in *The Crier* that tracks activities in the Market and in downtown Portland. The fall issue, for example, advertised the city's "Halloween Downtown" parade. This kind of outreach underscores and strengthens the secondary agenda of the Market: to be an important gathering space for residents of the Portland area, and to bring together different segments of the population in an ongoing effort to build and strengthen community.

FINANCING

Building Costs

The lion's share of the capital for the project came from Elizabeth Noyce and the Libra Foundation, but vendors and the City of Portland have also contributed, vendors to the tune of $1.1 million for stall improvements and equipment, and the City adding $250,000 in streetscape improvements including sidewalks, streetlamps, and crosswalks. Noyce contributed the land and nearly $9 million for construction and site work including the remediation of contaminated soils (see table below). Because of the percentage of gross sales component of each vendor's lease, the Libra Foundation could see a financial return if sales are high. One other player in the financing has been Coastal Enterprises, a nonprofit community development agency that helped finance several Market ventures. The agency funded Doug Ewart's "Out of the Blue" value-added seafood venture, for example, which sold salmon, scallop, and lobster sausages from a day table and then as a supplier to a permanent Market vendor.

BUILDING COST

	PROJECTION	ACTUAL
LAND ACQUISITION	0	0
SITE IMPROVEMENTS:		
SOIL REMEDIATION AND SITE WORK		851,129
DEMOLITION		41,545
SUBTOTAL:	**278,763**	**892,674**
CONSTRUCTION:		
BASE BUILDING (SEE TEXT BELOW FOR EXPLANATION)	3,116,961	6,093,866
TENANT IMPROVEMENTS		
DEVELOPER CONTRIBUTION	600,000	522,161
VENDOR CONTRIBUTION (STALL FIT-OUT)		1,100,000
PROFESSIONAL FEES	184,955	951,487
SUBTOTAL:	**3,901,916**	**8,667,514**
OTHER:		
SIGNAGE		$153,133
CAPITAL / EQUIPMENT		$206,482
INSURANCE FOR OWNER		7,748
OPENING PROMOTION	$80,000	60,000
OTHER	$350,000	11,632
SUBTOTAL:	$430,000	438,995
TOTAL:	4,610,679	9,999,183

Building the Market cost significantly more than Spitzer's original projections (see table above), partly as the result of three major plan changes. First, the square footage was expanded into portions of the parking lot of the nearby public library to provide more "back stage" space for storage, kitchens, and so forth. Then air conditioning, which had initially been cut from the project as an economy move, was brought back in with modified rooftop units. Finally, the parking garage was connected to the Market by an enclosed skybridge to help offset customers' dislike of parking garages. (The skybridge is now the most used entrance to the Market.)

Vendor Leases

The Selection Committee was particularly impressed with the lease system for vendors, which was based on Spitzer's studies of other public markets. The lease lengths were determined in large part by the tenant's investment in equipment and fit-out and his or her previous retailing experience. The fit-out for farmers' stalls was subsidized to encourage participation. Lease structures also favor farmers and producer-prepared foods over ordinary retail (see table below). Together, these rental structures help create incentives for vendors to do well while serving as an incubator protecting those still faring poorly. They also contribute to a robust organizational structure that the Selection Committee felt stood a good chance of maintaining its values if and when the Market undergoes further changes in leadership.

Unlike some public markets, the lease rate system is fairly simple, consisting of three parts: a common area maintenance (CAM) charge; a base rent or a 4-8% portion of gross sales, whichever is higher; and a share of parking expenses. The average rent is approximately $2,000 per month, or up to $40 per net square foot, as compared to about $25 per gross square foot in Old Port. Both management and vendors anticipate that the relatively high square-foot rent will be offset by high volumes and synergies with other vendors.

To keep track of gross sales, all of the permanent vendors are tied together in a central point-of-sale system. This system not only removes any incentive to misrepresent sales, but also provides an excellent base of data about sales patterns for the Market as a whole. Market management uses this information as an early warning system to determine if one vendor is falling behind relative to others and also shares the data with the tenants so they can have points of comparison for their own analysis. Unlike any other public market, the centralized POS system gives management an accurate "pulse" of the Market as a whole.

The universal point-of-sale cash register system has already been helpful in this regard during the summer. By closely watching each vendor's sales levels and rents, it became clear that rents were higher, as a percentage of gross sales, than Spitzer felt was sustainable for the vendors. Based on this analysis, the Market decided to lower CAM charges for a period of 12 months. This decision effectively lowered rents, which were averaging about 10% of gross sales, to about 8.5%, which had been the original target. Daytable rates have also been lowered, in some cases by a full 50% (see table below). Spitzer plans to monitor these levels continually and make adjustments to help the vendors achieve profitability while also meeting income requirements.

DAY TABLES RATES (before and after rate decreases)

WEEKENDS	4-9-99	1-1-00	4-9-99	1-1-00	4-9-99	1-1-00
PRODUCER $40	$20	$60	$30	$75	$60	
NON-PRODUCER	$50	$30	$70	$40	$90	$90
WEEKDAYS						
PRODUCER $20	$10	$30	$20	$50	$40	
NON-PRODUCER	$30	$20	$40	$30	$60	$60

At this stage, the parking system has not yet been fully worked out. At first there was a validation system, where customers could have their tickets stamped after spending five dollars; the vendors would then pay based on the number of tickets they had stamped. But this system created problems for shoppers who spent less than five dollars at each stall. The Market temporarily agreed to pay for all validated tickets while a new system was put into place. Now, vendors pay a fixed fee based on their percentage of total Market sales. The intent, clearly, is to have customers park free and to equitably share parking costs across the market.

Revenue

The Market itself is not yet expected to turn a profit, but Wells hopes it will be self-sufficient after a few years of operation. First year gross sales for all Market vendors exceeded sales goals of $6 million, with more than half the vendors surpassing their initial sales estimates, some by a factor of three. After a slow start, weekly sales had nearly reached the level of the grand opening by the end of the summer. Ironically, the slow start may have been due to exceptionally good summer weather. As one Market farmer put it, "I thought I was getting *out* of the weather business!" Additionally, although sales were good, all vendors continued to struggle with the lack of available labor in the region, a situation that has driven up wages and production costs. Nonetheless, only two out of the 21 original permanent vendors decided to leave the Market, and those two were replaced by five new businesses, leaving a year-end total of 24 vendors.

The feasibility study estimated that the Market should be capable of achieving $10 million in sales in a mature environment. Total operating costs are running at about $720,000 per year. An extensive customer survey undertaken in 1999 reveals the accuracy of Spitzer's initial feasibility study. In particular, the importance of customers from the ring within 30 minutes of downtown Portland became very clear. As predicted, tourists have represented about 15% of the customers since opening.

THE MARKET AND THE CITY OF PORTLAND

The City of Portland played a relatively minor role in the development of the Market, but had been working hard at creating mechanisms for encouraging commercial development in the downtown. Low-interest loans for commercial and retail venues, a \$1.2 million package to bring the Maine College of Art to the Porteous Department Store space, and other incentives contributed to creating an atmosphere conducive to development. The Portland Public Market, while not part of the City's arts corridor and Old Port plans, enhanced the City's efforts by connecting the two ends of the downtown spine with a central destination.

Although the City was cooperative on the various approvals required by the Market, many officials were concerned about traffic, and shared the general skepticism about the Market's chances for success. Those reservations notwithstanding, however, the City was supportive of the Market, investing \$250,000 in sidewalk improvements and lighting around the building. Additionally, the Downtown Business Improvement District provided a subtle subsidy by extending its snow and trash removal and cleaning services beyond its existing boundaries to the Market. The District is a private organization supported by assessments to business and property owners. Its contribution of services is a significant boost to the Market, and life in the Market adds to the vitality of the District.

IMPACT ON THE CITY

Thirty years ago, says Sam Ladd of the Maine Bank & Trust, Portland's downtown was alive and well; ten years ago it was a wasteland. While the Public Market cannot take all the credit for a more recent turnaround, which began with Noyce's other philanthropic ventures in the city center, the project has clearly been kind to the city. In the early 1990s, vacancy rates in office buildings ranged from 40% to 90%. "Old Port," the tourist area, basically drove what remained of the city, and the Congress Street area proved unable to draw any activity. Recovery began as Noyce purchased buildings near Monument Square, and by 1996 the downtown had achieved an 86% occupancy rate. Even so, John Costa of L.L. Bean remembers the early days when Congress Street attracted panhandlers and shoplifters along with shoppers. Now, he reports, the street is lively, he has days at 50% over the daily budget, and business overall has improved 10%. He attributes these gains to the draw of the Market, which brings 10-15,000 people per week to the downtown.

The Market has been a boon in any number of other ways as well. Ladd notes that conditions on Preble Street were "awful" before the new development, basically just an empty parking lot and vacant buildings. The Market spurred the City to invest money in improving the streetscapes around Preble Street. A flower garden in Mrs. Noyce's memory has been installed on Preble directly behind the Maine Bank & Trust. At the commercial level, businesses are moving back into the area at a rapid pace; for example, a wine merchant and mortgage facility have located across Preble Street in renovated buildings. And at the cultural level, the Market has augmented and is helping extend the arts district. It helps connect the district to the Old Port tourist center and helps make it unique by adding what vendors variously call "food theater" and "bread art" – which is to say, not just food for sale but educational "performances" on where the food comes from, highlighting Maine's agricultural tradition. The Museum Director says the Market has also spurred a 15% rise in attendance at the Portland Museum of Art, already one of the nation's highest per-capita membership museums.

The Market's L-shaped plan gives it street frontage on three sides with good daylight at all hours.

The Market, in sum, has accelerated and intensified a general recovery aided by Noyce's philanthropic activities. It has brought activity, commerce, and excitement back to the downtown, increasing traffic enormously and spurring the formation of a neighborhood association and what former Portland Mayor George Campbell calls a "sense of community and constituency" in the previously moribund Bayside neighborhood. The neighborhood association has reactivated and is now focusing its energies on the proposed sports and entertainment center (on land donated by the Libra Foundation). It also tries to fend off gentrification, prevent dislocation of agencies and elderly residents, and ensure that any demolished housing stock will be replaced. In general, as one vendor put it, Bayside has become the "hot new area in town," a "good place to take a gamble."

FUTURE PLANS

The Portland Public Market is still a relatively young project. It has been in operation only since October 1998 and had not at the time of our visit experienced a summer's growing season and tourist trade. Plans for the immediate future are therefore still focused on full implementation of original goals. Management is working to increase visibility and patronage by "getting the word out," working with tourist agencies to incorporate the Market on tourist routes, and working with vendors to improve the marketing and display of their food. The Market is relatively free from economic pressure as it is only expected to break even on operating costs. Profit above and beyond this reverts to the Libra Foundation.

In the next year the Market will build out the remaining unfinished space at the far end of the building, just below the management office. This space is designated for restaurant use, and will provide an anchor at the opposite end of the Market from Hanson Brothers' Seafood Cafe. Because there is already a seating area in this corner of the market, and a specialty Italian food vendor nearby, a restaurant will further enliven the area and provide balanced restaurant destinations at either end of the L-shaped space.

Eave detail

ASSESSING PROJECT SUCCESS

HOW WELL PROJECT MEETS ITS OWN GOALS

- *To help revitalize downtown Portland by creating a magnet that will attract individuals and families from throughout the region, downtown workers, and tourists, and thereby strengthen center city retail.*

The Market has made a promising start on this goal, with nearby buildings being restored and put to use, many customers coming to the market, and an aura of excitement and optimism taking hold of the downtown area. The strengthening of Portland's "spine" promises to aid in the success of future revitalization efforts like the Civic Center. As most vendors concede, it is still too soon to tell how steady business will be once the novelty wears off, but the project has been very carefully planned and well executed. At this point, it appears to be headed in the right direction.

- *To provide economic opportunity for small business people.*

Because of the lease structure and the Market's outreach programs, more than two-thirds of the vendors are farmers or food producers. All are locally owned family businesses. Even though the success rate of these ventures cannot yet be ascertained, there can be no doubt that opportunities have been provided; as one vendor opined, "success is up to us; if it works, it will be because we did it right."

- *To expand on the success of the existing farmers market and thereby strengthen agriculture in the region.*

While it is not yet clear what impact the Market has had on Maine's agriculture, it has at the very least provided a compelling model for struggling small farmers to follow as they try to bring the state's farming industry back from the brink of collapse. It has been particularly important as an example of vertical integration and specialty marketing, a key strategy for relatively small-scale producers with high production costs. It has also helped highlight the state program to encourage residents to buy locally. Finally, outdoor farmers' market vendors have seen increased traffic.

- *To create a place where people from Portland's various social and ethnic groups mix freely and where the region's multi-ethnic food and agricultural traditions are celebrated.*

Although it is difficult to get a grasp of Portland's "various social and ethnic groups," all indications are that this goal is being met. Mark Swann remarks that Preble Street clients can be seen "shopping and grazing" through the market (which is dotted with inviting free samples). Graphics celebrate Maine agricultural traditions, and a good many vendors engage in "food theater" by dramatizing the origins of the food they are selling. As Smiling Hill Farm vendor Roger Knight explains, "We are attractive to customers who want to be closer to the food chain."

OTHER MEASURES OF SUCCESS

Adaptability / Replicability

The Portland Public Market represents yet another successful application of the flexible public market template. This has been, in part, the result of Spitzer's long experience and skills in market development – and certainly has been aided by Spitzer's inclusive leadership style – but it also reflects the basic utility of the public market concept. The idea has already been proven to work in other locales, adapting to a variety of local conditions and designed to meet a wide range of local needs. The Rudy Bruner Award's own archives reflect the value of the public market concept; Seattle's Pike Place Market was selected as the 1987 Gold Medal Winner, and New York's Greenmarket was a 1991 Silver Medalist (See "For Further Information" below). Pike Place Market, in particular, has been an important prototype for efforts in other cities, and many Pike Place innovations can be found in the Portland Market.

Values Reflected in Development Process

Economic development through private philanthropy has clearly been the central value of this project. The process involves money coming almost entirely from a single private philanthropist, and design and construction coming from professional architects, engineers, and construction managers. However, the commitment to include local materials and craftsmen and to revitalize local and regional economies – in particular, the downtown and small family farms – has given the process a distinct identity.

Like many Rudy Bruner Award winners, its successes have come from balancing what may appear to be inhospitable elements: the needs of small farmers; the needs of economically disadvantaged residents of the central city; the needs of grocery shoppers; and the desires of tourists. The vision behind this successful balancing is one that sees the complementary possibilities of different constituencies, hoping that together they can overcome a wide array of problems not amenable to individual solutions.

Overall, the Selection Committee was impressed by the Market, recognizing its financial competence, its social values, its attractiveness as a shopping destination, and its contribution to downtown revitalization. They also, however, recognized that the project had a significant head start over most urban interventions because of the philanthropy of Elizabeth Noyce. Thus, while the Selection Committee lauded the Market for its successes, they felt that the project had not had to overcome many common obstacles to development, thus creating a question about how useful a model Portland's experience can be. Nonetheless, as one Committee member noted, the amount of money involved was relatively small in relation to the significant impact the Market has had on Portland. Lack of a wealthy philanthropist should not be an insurmountable obstacle for other cities interested in creating a public market, and its commitment to the local and regional economy remain impressive.

FOR FURTHER INFORMATION

Theodore Spitzer and Hilary Baum, *Public Markets and Community Revitalization* (Washington, DC: Urban Land Institute and Project for Public Spaces, Inc., 1995). *A "how-to" oriented survey of the nature, benefits, challenges, planning, development, management, feasibility, operations, and evolution of public markets co-written by the Portland Public Market's own Ted Spitzer. Features case study examples from Pike Place, Pasco Farmers', El Mercado, East Orange Community, Bronx Sunday, and North Markets.*

Nancy Fox, "Case study: Pike Place Market, Seattle," in Bernard J. Frieden and Lynne B. Sagalyn, eds., *Downtown, Inc.: How America Rebuilds Cities* (Cambridge, MA: MIT Press, 1989).

Meadow Rue Merrill, "Portland project will give farm goods a gourmet touch," *Boston Sunday Globe,* (August 16, 1998, pp. B10, B12).

Related Rudy Bruner Award Winners

(For a full bibliographic cites, please see Introduction)

Pike Place Market, Seattle (1987 cycle). The complexity of goods and services, the mixture of merchants and farmers, the co-existence of boutiques and second-hand stores, and the democratic processes that created a living community out of a public market.

Greenmarket, New York City (1991 cycle). A system of more than a dozen New York City farmer's markets that helped revive Union Square, created a warm, sociable neighborhood, and supported the survival of the small, family-owned New York farm.

Contact

Portland Public Market
Ted Spitzer, Director
25 Preble Street, Suite 200
Portland, ME 04101
Phone: 207-228-2004
Web: http://www.portlandmarket.com/

RUDY BRUNER AWARD FOR URBAN EXCELLENCE

BRUNER FOUNDATION
130 Prospect Street
Cambridge, MA 02139
PH: 617.492.8404
FX: 617.876.4002

www.brunerfoundation.org

1999 Rudy Bruner Award

SILVER

medal winner

NATIONAL AIDS MEMORIAL GROVE

San Francisco, California

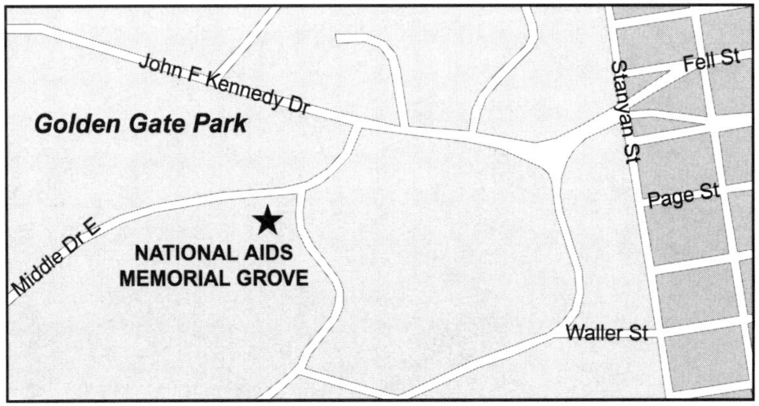
John F Kennedy Dr
Golden Gate Park
Middle Dr E
NATIONAL AIDS
MEMORIAL GROVE
Stanyan St
Fell St
Page St
Waller St

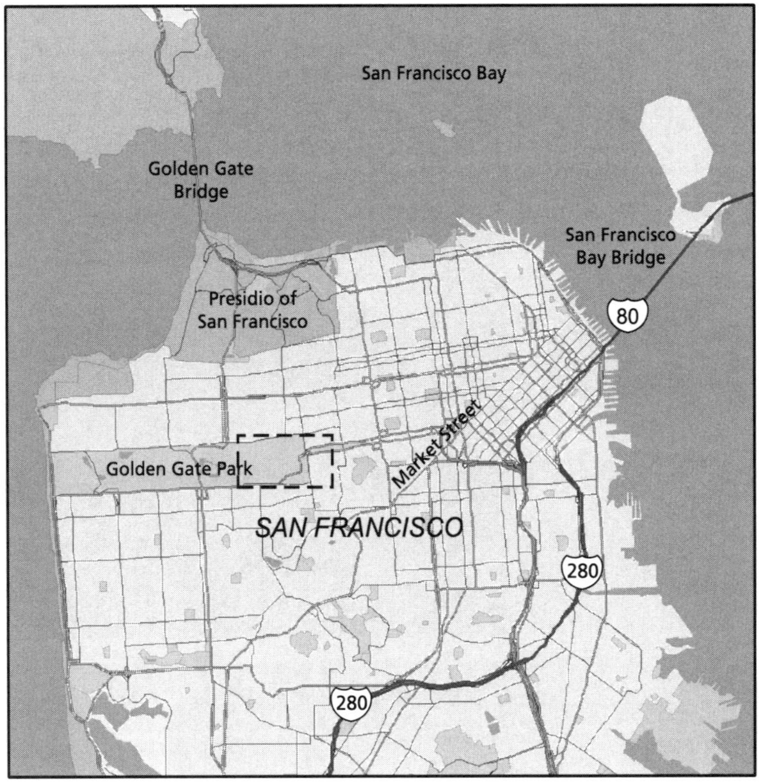
San Francisco Bay
Golden Gate
Bridge
San Francisco
Bay Bridge
Presidio of
San Francisco
80
Golden Gate Park
Market Street
SAN FRANCISCO
280
280

NATIONAL AIDS MEMORIAL GROVE AT A GLANCE

WHO MADE THE SUBMISSION?

- National AIDS Memorial Grove; Thom Weyand, Executive Director.

WHAT IS THE NATIONAL AIDS MEMORIAL GROVE?

- A living memorial for the use and benefit of the public and especially of all people whose lives have been touched by the AIDS epidemic.

- A 7.5-acre dell in the east end of Golden Gate Park, formerly derelict and unused, which has been restored and re-integrated into the Park for enjoyment by the public.

- A venue for monthly volunteer workdays that bring together many communities to build and maintain the Grove, to remember those who have died by participating in a monthly ritual, and to provide comfort and support to the living.

- A national memorial of the loss caused by AIDS in San Francisco and around the country.

- A public-private partnership that has secured public parkland on a long-term basis, that has generated ongoing community stewardship, and whose maintenance is intended to be funded in perpetuity.

NATIONAL AIDS MEMORIAL GROVE

CHRONOLOGY

1988
Small group convenes to discuss creating a living memorial for those who have died of AIDS.

1989-1990
Discussion begins with Golden Gate Park about designating an appropriate space.

1991
De Laveaga Dell, an overgrown, neglected 7.5-acre space in the east end of the park, is selected. Cleaning and weeding begins at groundbreaking, launching monthly volunteer workdays. Capital campaign (Circle of Friends) begins.

1994
A 99-year lease agreement signed with San Francisco Recreation and Park Department. An endowment to cover the gardener's salary and maintenance becomes a goal.

1996
Congress and the President confer national status on the Grove (the only AIDS memorial so designated).

1998
Phase II of endowment campaign (Ensure Remembrance) commences.

KEY PARTICIPANTS

Individuals who were interviewed are marked with an asterisk [*]

Grove Administrative Staff

*Thom Weyand, Executive Director, NAMG

Board of Directors

*Alice Russell-Shapiro, Board of Directors
David Linger, Founding Chair, Board of Directors
*Jack Porter, Board of Directors
*Larry Colton, Board of Directors
*Gina Gatta, Board of Directors
Mike Kurokawa, Board of Directors
*Len Weise, Board of Directors

US Government

*Hon. Nancy Pelosi, Congresswoman

City of San Francisco

*Deborah Learner, Park Planner, San Francisco Recreation and Park Department
*Joan Vellutini, Gardener, San Francisco Recreation and Park Department
*Mark Leno, Supervisor

- 1988 — Small group conceives memorial concept
- 1990 — Discussions with Golden Gate Park begin
- 1991 — DeLaveaga Dell selected
- 1991 — Work begins on site clean-up
- 1994 — 99 year lease signed with Park Dept.
- 1996 — Grove designated as National Memorial

Designers

*Michael Boland, Designer, Past Board Member
*Ira Kurlander, Designer, Board of Directors
*Connie de Laveaga Stoops, Architect, Past Board Member
*Clare Cooper Marcus, early participant
Michael Enguidanos, Project Manager, hardscape installation
William Peters, Past Board Member

Volunteers

*Elaine Shen, Volunteer
*Carlin Holden, Volunteer

Fiscal Agent

Justin Probert, The Tides Center (fiscal agent)

Pink umbrellas decorate the grove for National AIDS Awareness Day.

PROJECT DESCRIPTION

HISTORY

"It was an idea born out of desperation. We all felt the need for a place where people could find solace, solidarity, and hope—and the sense of renewal that is inspired by nature."
Alice Russell-Shapiro, Co-founder and Board Co-chair.

The AIDS Memorial Grove grew out of the response of a small group of people to the overwhelming devastation wrought by the AIDS epidemic on the San Francisco gay community. Early participants included Alice Russell-Shapiro, Isabel Wade, and Nancy McNally, all of whom had worked with urban environmental groups including the Trust for Public Land, Friends of the Urban Forest, and other organizations. They were joined by landscape designer Stephen Marcus (who was then afflicted with AIDS and knew he did not have long to live), David Linger, and Jim Hormel. This initial group conceived of creating a place that would memorialize those who had died, increase public awareness of the crisis, and be a beautiful public space for remembering and reflecting. They wanted to create "something organic, something life-affirming" to counteract the ravages of the epidemic. Meeting informally in 1988 and 1989, the group originally envisioned a "gingko grove," with a tree planted for each AIDS death. As the proportions of the epidemic grew, and as the group gained knowledge and sophistication, their vision of the grove evolved into a public open space that would allow for quiet contemplation, gatherings, and remembrance not only for those affected by AIDS but for the general public as well.

In 1989, the Committee began searching for a site. Negotiations with the San Francisco Recreation and Park Department started in earnest that same year. After reviewing several options, the group selected Golden Gate Park because of its national stature, accessibility, and familiarity to the diverse communities affected by the AIDS epidemic. In addition, a Golden Gate Park site would increase the chances of the Grove gaining the kind of visibility the group was seeking.

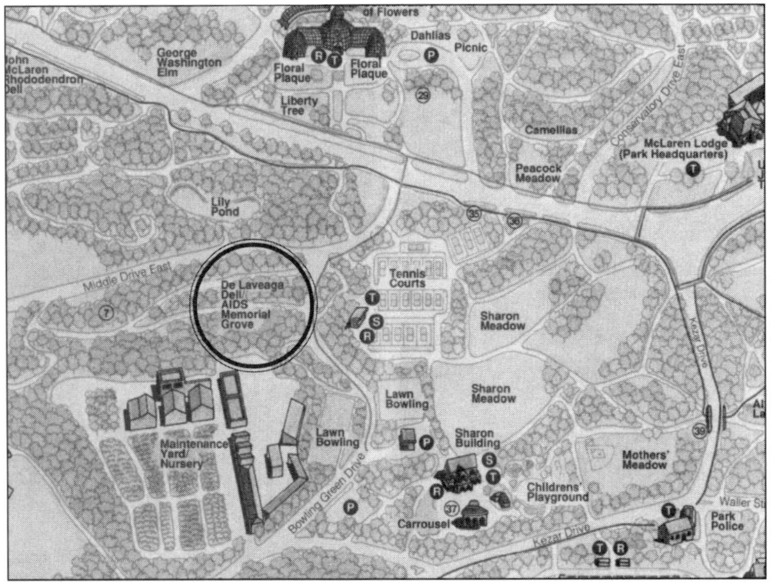

The AIDS Memorial Grove in the east end of Golden Gate Park

Golden Gate Park planners were skeptical at first. Proponents of the Grove, however, had gained credibility through their planning and fundraising, and promised not only to reclaim a significant area in the park but to fund a gardener to maintain the area in perpetuity. On the strength of that commitment, the Park authorities accepted the proposal and identified six possible sites. De Laveaga Dell, at the east end of the Park, was ultimately selected.

De Laveaga Dell, given to the park by the de Laveaga family in the1890s and landscaped in 1921, was one of the oldest developed parts of Golden Gate Park, but it had been seriously neglected since the early 1980s due to budget cuts. As family members who had been saddened by this neglect recall, the policy seemed to be "If you can't see it from the car, it doesn't matter." The Dell was prominently located on a major park drive, but occupied a low-lying area separated from the road by embankments overgrown with brambles and berries. Drainage problems in the meadow below had resulted in frequent flooding. Due in part to its lack of visibility from the road and pathways above, the Dell had become a haven for the homeless and for drug users, and was considered one of the most dangerous areas in the Park.

The 7.5-acre site offered the kind of topography, size, and location the AIDS Memorial Grove advocates were seeking. The de Laveaga family's enthusiasm for the proposal was an added bonus. The family was eager to see the Dell revived, had lost a family member to AIDS, and felt sympathetic to the aims of the Grove. A further coincidence was that Connie de Laveaga Stoops, a great-niece of Jose Vicente de Laveaga, who had given the Dell to the City, was then an architecture student who was willing to become involved in the project. An informal agreement to use de Laveaga Dell was reached in 1991.

September 19, 1991 marked the first workday and is considered the birthday of the Grove. Two hundred people attended that day, inaugurating many months of labor-intensive weed, tree, and bramble removal. These early workdays were recalled vividly by participants like Congresswoman Nancy Pelosi, Supervisor Mark Leno, and the Board members. Everyone agreed that the state of deterioration of the site was in some ways an apt metaphor for the impact of the AIDS epidemic – reclamation seemed a daunting prospect.

In 1994 the AIDS Memorial Grove officially leased the de Laveaga Dell from Golden Gate Park for 99 years, promising in return to maintain the site, and ultimately to fund a full-time gardener in perpetuity. The funding process began with a significant personal contribution from each member of the newly formed Board and a seed grant from the Columbia Foundation, and continued with campaigns to pay for construction and to endow the gardener position by offering opportunities for donors to inscribed names on tasteful monuments in the Grove (See "Finances" below).

Workday volunteers build and maintain the Grove

Workday volunteer

VISION

The Grove and the volunteer workdays that built and maintain it have been guided by a central vision that speaks in important ways to the nature and purpose of memorials. To begin with, the Grove was intentionally designed with local conditions and communities in mind. Renewing the abandoned Dell and providing a place for all San Franciscans touched by the AIDS epidemic were the original concerns; national status came later as an unexpected addition. As Representative Nancy Pelosi pointed out to the site visit team, San Francisco is a particularly appropriate location for an AIDS memorial because the city's tolerance and openness have long made it a home for the nation's gay and lesbian communities. As such, it has not only become an important symbolic and organizational center for those communities, but it has been one of the cities hardest-hit by the AIDS epidemic. As a result of San Francisco's important role in gay and lesbian life, the Grove was able to build on an already existing grassroots network of support and participation. This vision of serving a local community has been crucial to the Grove's success in attaining broader recognition.

A second element of the Grove's animating vision is the concept of a *living* memorial, one that renews and rebuilds as well as remembers. At its most basic level this is evidenced by the choice of the neglected Dell: as the Dell needed to be restored, so too did those affected by the AIDS epidemic. The acts of organizing, volunteering, and creating the Grove were, and continue to be, part of the healing process, creating a living testimony to renewal. In the words of Michael Boland, "The community's role in the act of creation was a critical part of the Grove's healing function. Although the Grove is for the most part 'built' in the conventional sense of the word, it continues to be *created* as a result of community activity at the site." Representative Nancy Pelosi added that the clearing of the Grove was a metaphor for dealing with AIDS: it seemed a hopeless task in the beginning, but as they made progress, they brought light to the Grove and also to the subject of AIDS. Not coincidentally, the end result of these life-affirming activities is itself a living thing, composed of plants and animals that will also continue to grow and mature over time; meditation and remembrance can take place at the memorial without a funereal atmosphere.

Old Live Coast Oak overhangs the path to the Fern Grotto

Related to the Grove's status as a living memorial is its role as a facilitating site for activities and organizations working on AIDS issues. It is a venue for delivering AIDS policy statements, and nonprofit AIDS organizations use it for receptions and fundraising. It annually hosts the pre-eminent World AIDS Day event in the Bay Area. It also serves as an educational forum for teaching about a wide range of AIDS issues, particularly since its adoption by schools and youth volunteer organizations as a site to send young volunteers. Thus the Grove remains dynamic in its creation and composition as well as in its ongoing affirmation of life.

ORGANIZATION AND LEADERSHIP

The Grove's formal organization consists of a 14-member Board of Directors and an administrative staff that includes the Executive Director, the Volunteer Program Manager, and the Office Manager. Technically the Board is an advisory body, inasmuch as nonprofit status is held by the Tides Foundation, which serves as fiscal agent for the Grove. Thom Weyand, hired in late 1997, is the second Executive Director, and comes to the Grove with an impressive background in fundraising for nonprofit enterprises. He also has significant experience working with the gay community, including service as Development Director of the AIDS Memorial Quilt.

The original plan for the organization was to build the Grove, fulfill the fundraising obligations contained in the Golden Gate Park agreement, and then disband. Many original Board members remain involved and active, however, and are still committed to the early goals. As the functions of the Grove become more complex, the need for an ongoing organization is becoming clearer.

Efforts are underway to increase the visibility of the Grove. Nine new Board members include professionals in the field of marketing and communication who have produced a new plan for increasing awareness of the Grove (see "Future Plans" below). Other issues such as nonprofit status, evaluation and direction of maintenance and design, and administration of workdays suggest the need for continued administration of the Grove by an advocacy organization. These issues and others were the subject of an April, 1999 Board retreat, which established a Long Range Vision committee to study future organizational needs.

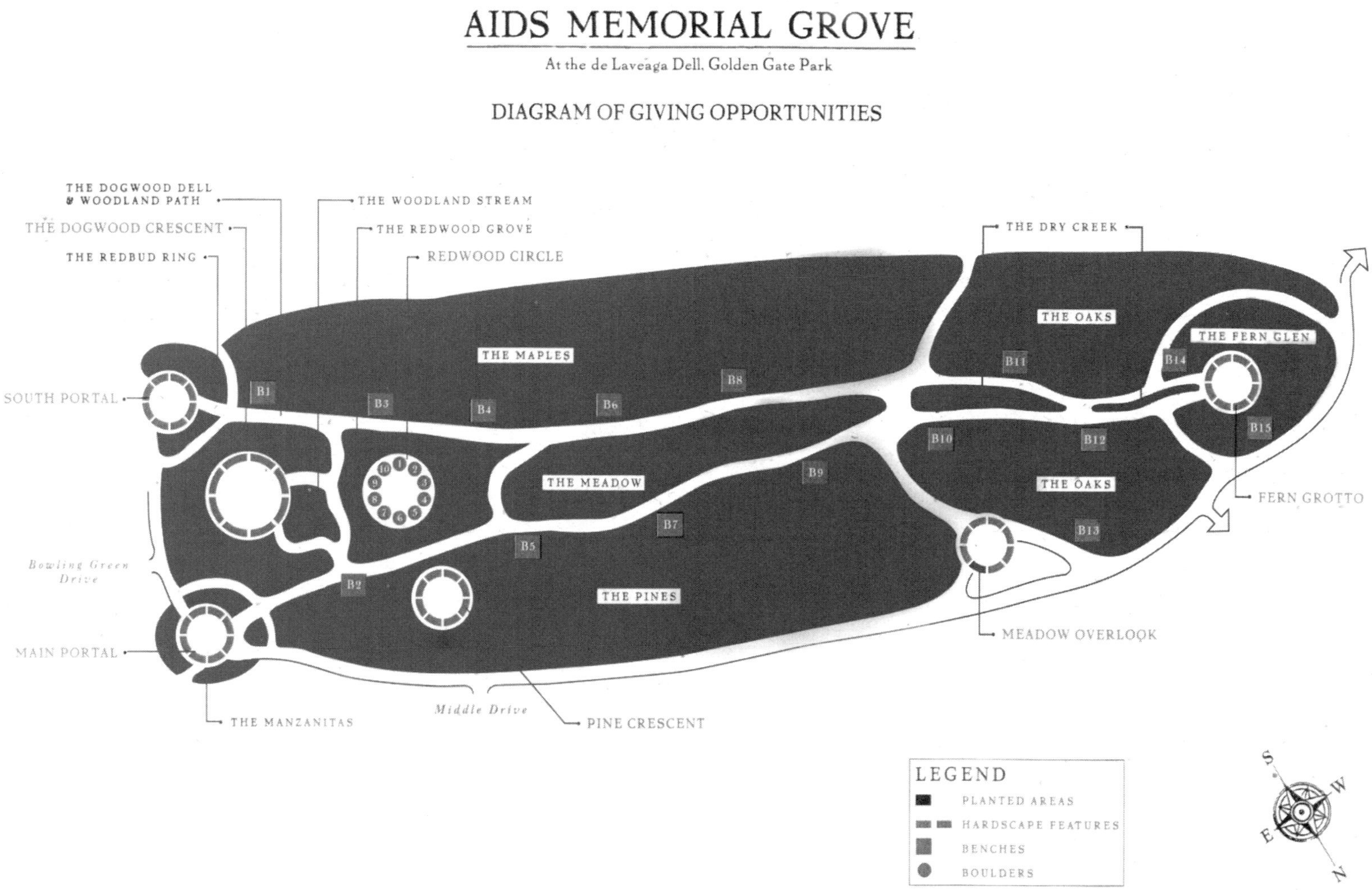

The site plan for the Aids Memorial Grove reveals a longitudinal form and a range of small and large spaces.

DESIGN

Many of the original Grove founders were practicing architects and landscape architects. Among them were Michael Boland, a landscape architect who became the designer of record; Ira Kurlander, an architect who remains on the Board today; William Peters, a landscape architect and former Board member; Todd Cole, a landscape architect; and Connie de Laveaga Stoops, also an architect and former Board member. Clare Cooper Marcus, a retired professor of landscape architecture at UC Berkeley, ex-wife of the late Stephen Marcus (one of the original Grove founders), also participated in the early design charettes. In addition, local designers such as Garrett Eckbo and Rod Freebairn-Smith participated in the design process and brainstormed about the form the Grove might take.

The original design group divided itself into three teams so that several different alternative plans could be considered. Each of the teams worked to develop a preliminary design that would embody the ideas that the group had been discussing for the past year or so. These early charettes were part of a lengthy and, in the words of the designers, "organic" design process that incorporated new ideas into an overall vision that was robust enough to absorb changes without becoming derailed. For example, the original gingko grove idea became a more elaborate park, and fundraising challenges were met with design changes that permitted more naming opportunities.

A Journey Through the Park

Two central themes emerged from these early design charettes, forming a conceptual framework for the final design. The first of these was the idea that a journey through the Grove should be a metaphor for the struggle with AIDS by both victims and survivors. The journey begins with the descent from the light and activity of the street into a secluded and shadowed area, and then moves through darkness and shadow – isolation – to eventual re-emergence into the light. The second theme is the Grove as a sacred and silent space for reflection apart from the city. With portals to define entrances, the longitudinal form of the bowl, and the inclusion of gathering spaces as well as places for solitude, the Grove is a kind of cathedral, its quiet yet powerful aura underlying the spiritual experience. Both of these design stories incorporate a vocabulary of round and broken round forms – circles, a Board member explained, that get broken when people die.

A large boulder marks the east entrance to the Grove.

Dry creek bed leading out to the meadow

Balancing these very serious thematic concepts are a variety of elements designed to make the Grove feel welcoming and peaceful. The meadow at the center, clearly visible from the sidewalks above, creates a tranquil and safe place for children and other visitors. The beige Minnesota flagstone selected for the Circle of Friends at the east entry, for the Fern Grotto at the west entry, and for the Pine Crescent near the center of the Grove was chosen for its light and warm color. These hardscape elements are penetrable by pathways from several directions, and form "destination" points at either end of the Grove. Movement is further facilitated by granite curbstone (donated by the city) used throughout the park, serving as erosion-control barriers and as pathways. Wide stair-like pathways lead up and down from the sidewalk above into the Grove itself. Plants are a combination of native flora such as Redwoods (whose numbers have risen thanks to volunteers); the Coast Live Oaks that form the central showpiece of the Fern Grotto pathway; native Sword Fern; Clivea; and other plants that are prominent around Golden Gate Park. Infestations of several pests are threatening the Monterey pines, so other more resistant varieties are slowly being introduced. Plant species have been selected with an eye toward having something in bloom throughout the year.

Above and beyond design considerations, the group faced the challenge of creating a memorial that communicated the magnitude of loss from the epidemic, yet did not feel like a graveyard. It strove to be life-affirming in the face of the terrible losses, and to give a sense of hope and community amidst the crisis. In that respect, it was important that the names in the Circle of Friends remain muted, almost pattern-like. The names were intended to communicate a strong but subtle presence, there for those who come across them, or who are looking for the name of a loved one, but not dominating the space, which was intended for use by the public as well. The significance of the names is announced tastefully at the entrance to the Circle, in a poem-like message engraved on the small bridge: "Circle of Friends / Lives Touched By AIDS / Donors To The Grove / Those Who Have Died / Those Who Loved Them." The site visit team and Selection Committee agreed that the Grove successfully avoided the feel of a cemetery, both because of the site's usage patterns (especially the workdays) and the relative subtlety of the name placements and explanation. However, the Selection Committee wondered whether this subtlety might be a two-edged sword. In the future, a Committee member asked, when AIDS has been cured, will the memorial aspect of the Dell be obvious to visitors?

The site visit team felt that the Grove achieved its goal of creating a place with a tangible sense of spirituality. It is, they reported, a contemplative place that can provide a platform for many kinds of commemoration and remembrance. Clare Cooper Marcus, for example, showed photographs of a leaf design that she and her children created on the trunk of the Coast Live Oak at the west end of the Grove. She described it as an ephemeral memorial, something she creates yearly with her children in memory of their father. For her, these kinds of highly personal gestures are appropriate and meaningful for connecting with the cycle of life, death, and rebirth.

Other personal gestures were evident at the site visit – bouquets left at the Circle of Friends, for example, or a stone adorned with a first name left in the former creek bed. It is just such simple, small-scale rituals for which the Grove was designed; as designer Ira Kurlander explained, their goal was not to "dazzle everyone with our virtuosity" but to create a subtle, humble place that would facilitate without interfering.

The site visit team also reported some disappointments in the Grove's design. The Selection Committee agreed that the Grove presents locations of striking beauty but also houses areas of lesser quality. Additionally, when viewed as a whole, the Committee felt that the Grove did not appear as inspiring as some of the details

Names carved in the Circle of Friends

Stone carving identifying the site of the Circle of Friends.

could lead one to expect. They raised questions about the placement of and relationships between hardscape and organic elements, and also noted the lack of a central monument – something that has been debated among the Grove's own designers as well. Michael Boland, for example, has voiced a lingering frustration that the Grove does not make a stronger statement about the numbers lost to AIDS; he would have liked to "turn up the volume" and create something that more effectively communicates the enormity of the crisis. The Selection Committee agreed with Boland, remarking that the lack of a "signature statement" of some sort added to the Grove's tendency towards over-subtlety, robbing it of the strength and evocation of other national monuments like the Vietnam War Memorial. Consideration is still being given at the Board level to introducing some sort of "marker" near the west end of the Grove, to further commemorate those lost to the epidemic.

The Dogwood Crescent

Ephemerel, personal memorials can be as simple as this small rock sculpture.

Americans with Disabilities Act (ADA)

The Grove and its designers have some ongoing issues with respect to ADA, a law created for indoor spaces and not yet fully interpreted in its application to the outdoors. At one of the east entrances, the Grove has designed and built a handsome, winding wheelchair ramp that leads to the Dogwood Crescent. Designers and Grove Board and staff are sensitive to the need for the Grove to be fully accessible, as many visitors are sick or wheelchair-bound. At the center of the Grove, however, the Pine Crescent, reached by a pathway and a stepped path, is not fully accessible. Similarly, the Fern Grotto at the western edge of the Grove is reached from somewhat steep paths on the meadow side, and stairs on the sidewalk end. Some kind of ramp or lift will be required to make the Grove accessible from this edge, and designers are currently struggling with this issue. In addition, Grove designers have used stepped terraces edged in granite block as erosion control devices at the sloped entry points and at the Pine Crescent. These terraced pathways also serve as stairs but are of questionable accessibility, because they do not meet the ADA stair riser/tread requirements. As the interpretation of ADA with respect to outdoor space continues to be refined, the NAMG will resolve these issues.

Ecology and Maintenance

Joan Vellutini, a Golden Gate Park gardener for 22 years, specifically requested the full-time Grove maintenance position. She showed obvious pride in the state of the Grove today, emphasizing the deplorable condition of the Dell prior to its rebirth. When the clearing began, Vellutini and other gardeners would frequently find

Erosion control stairs also serve as a rustic entry to the Grove.

used needles and syringes in the Grove; indeed, these would frequently be stuck into the hoses in an apparent gesture of protest. The entire meadow area was frequently under water before work on the Grove began. Since then, drainage tanks underneath the meadow have been repaired and improved, allowing for planting of grass. (As in other low-lying places in the Park, water is collected in the tank and pumped up to adjacent roadways, ultimately finding its way to the west end of the Park. Despite a recent $72-million bond issue that will provide funds to overhaul the antique infrastructure of Park irrigation systems, the Park is, and will remain, largely hand-watered.)

Meado Overlook sketch

Workdays: Planting, Maintenance, and Community Building

Originally conceived as an expedient way to involve people in the Grove and take advantage of much needed volunteer labor, workdays have become an important cornerstone of the memorial. Since 1991 thousands of volunteers have given more than 40,000 hours of their time at monthly (except in winter) workdays. This volunteer labor, together with the full-time gardener, keeps the Dell planted and maintained. There is unanimous agreement that workdays remain central to the meaning and strength of the Grove.

In the early 1990s workdays were attended by a core group of volunteers, many of whom were gay men, either HIV-positive or already suffering from AIDS. As the word spread about the Grove, others joined the effort, and the workdays grew and expanded. Over the years, as the Grove has become more fully built and treatment for AIDS has improved, the crisis nature of the epidemic has diminished and workdays have changed. Recent workdays have welcomed students, corporate groups, and youth volunteers from all over the Bay Area. Several corporations have played a particularly active role, including Charles Schwab and Company and the McKesson Corporation, joined by others such as the District Attorney's office and UC Medical Center. Many of these organizations have sent volunteers in memory of staff who died of AIDS. Others, like Levi Strauss, Bausch Chemicals, and Pacific Bell, have added "corporate volunteer days" to their financial contributions. This steady expansion of the Grove community is facilitated by the organization's quarterly newsletter, which as of our site visit had a circulation of 14,000.

Over the years, workdays have developed a predictable schedule and routine which provides not only the necessary labor, but also allows for moments of silence and sharing, giving deeper meaning to the experience. Volunteers arrive in the morning, are given a donated breakfast, and are organized into teams headed by experienced volunteers and sometimes by Golden Gate Park gardeners, several of whom donate their time to workdays. The volunteers work for several hours, then join the "circle of healing," a mid-day ritual described with obvious emotion by everyone who spoke about it. In it, organizers acknowledge volunteers for their efforts and accomplishments, poems or songs are shared, and community-related announcements can be made. Often Director Thom Weyand speaks briefly, and many have commented on his articulate and meaningful statements. The ritual is concluded with a short ceremony in which people are invited to "throw names into the circle." These names may be of loved ones lost, or persons suffering from or touched by AIDS. After each name there is a period of silence, and after the last name the group often plants a tree to commemorate their day. Finally, a generous lunch (also donated by local food businesses) is served before continuation of the work and cleanup.

Another important element of the workdays is their potential to broaden the base of understanding about gay and lesbian as well as AIDS issues. Elaine Shen, former Youth Volunteer Coordinator at the Volunteer Center of San Francisco, has sent youth groups to the Grove and other venues across city. The Grove, she maintains, did a good job of working with them, giving them important and productive work with visible results, and helping them to participate in something that made a difference. Even more notable, however, was the Grove's impact on the homophobia that Shen says "runs rampant" through this age group. Direct exposure to gay people and to people sick with AIDS has made a lasting impression on the attitudes of many young volunteers. The memorial provides one of the few venues available for young people of that age to get involved in working for an end to the epidemic. Many of Shen's youths have been inspired, she reports, and have become workday regulars.

The Grove's volunteer work days feature a mid-day ritual in which names of people to be remembered are "thrown" into a ceremonial circle.

Workday volunteers such as Congresswoman Nancy Pelosi have given literally thousands of hours to the Grove.

Perhaps the most intriguing aspect of the workdays is their power to foster community building. San Francisco, Shen explained, is a very "self-segregating" community despite its diversity. Workdays have been tremendously successful in bringing different racial, ethnic, and gender components of the community together, in part because AIDS recognizes no such boundaries. People who have lost siblings, children, and partners come together in workdays and have built strong and lasting bridges between those who might not otherwise have crossed paths. Shen was particularly impressed by the Grove's ability to attract young people of color, who she thought rarely felt connected to Golden Gate Park. It requires three bus transfers for many of them to get there (e.g., from Chinatown); without a structured opportunity they might not venture to that part of the city.

FINANCING

Walker within this circle, pause.
Although they all died of one cause,
Remember how their lives were dense
With fine, compacted difference.
Composed for Fern Grotto
by Thom Gunn, San Francisco poet

The Grove has been privately financed through a two-part fundraising campaign. The original capital campaign, Circle of Friends, funded the initial construction of the Grove. Its successor, the present-day Ensure Remembrance campaign, is focused primarily on raising an endowment. Co-chairs for the campaign include Ayse Kenmore, Alice Russell-Shapiro, Larry Colton, Jay Morton, and Christine Pelosi. The Circle of Friends was jump-started by five committed Board members who each donated $40,000 to the Grove. According to Board members, this initial financial commitment emboldened them to ask for larger donations from major philanthropists in the Bay Area, and provided adequate seed money to begin the clearing and building process.

To this end, the Board successfully raised $1.2 million for site improvements including the installation of eight flagstone gathering spots, 14 specially designed benches, a mobility access path, numerous Sierra granite boulders, two cobbled stream beds, and 17 individual planted areas. Private professional contractors were hired for the heavy construction, but volunteer workdays have supplied a significant portion of the labor (with an estimated value of $200,000). In addition, the City of San Francisco contributes significantly to the Grove by providing maintenance and some plant materials until the endowment goal is reached.

In the late 1990s, as AIDS treatment improved, and the crisis nature of the epidemic lessened somewhat, it became more difficult for the Grove and for other AIDS-related causes to secure needed funding. The new Executive Director, Thom Weyand, identified the need for a new approach to fundraising, and for a new capital campaign (Ensure Remembrance) to raise $1.7 million to fund the gardener position and any ongoing administrative functions required to sustain the Grove. The first $475,000 was raised relatively quickly through allowing larger corporate names to be inscribed in the outer circle of the Circle of Friends. Weyand has argued strongly, however, for the expansion of naming opportunities within the Grove to meet the campaign goals. Although this approach has been controversial, Weyand's arguments have been persuasive, and many new opportunities have now been identified (See "To Name or Not To Name," below).

The Grove has also completed a feasibility study for the second phase of the campaign, and those involved are "quite certain" that they can reach their goals on schedule. Current prospects have been identified and the Board is "cautiously optimistic" that many on the list will provide significant donations in 1999. The findings of the feasibility study support this conclusion and make some additional recommendations such as completing the campaign in the near future; raising the public profile of the Grove with innovative planning; continuing to clarify the audiences the Grove wishes to serve; and maintaining the commitment of strong and diverse leadership.

The annual distribution of income from the permanent $1.7 million endowment will be as follows:

ANNUAL DISTRIBUTION OF INCOME

$50,000	Annual Gardener Salary and Benefits
$25,000	Annual Maintenance and Upkeep
$15,000	Annual Repairs and Replacements
$90,000	(6% overall annual yield)

As the Grove has grown, so have management costs. The initial volunteer group has grown to include a small professional staff that runs the project full-time. Their tasks include project management, fundraising, workday and outreach coordination, planning, and special events. Costs are reflected in the Project Management Budget.

A brief financial summary as of close of fiscal year 1998 is as follows:

OVERVIEW OF NAMG FINANCES (12/98)

Grove construction	$1,455,000
Raised to date	$1,340,000
Remaining	$115,000
Endowment	$1,500,000
Raised to date	$675,000
Remaining	$875,000
Final phase project mgt	$1,075,000
Raised to date	$555,000
Remaining	$520,000
Total project costs	$4,030,000
Total funds raised	$2,570,000
TOTAL to be raised	**$1,135,000**

The Board has recently discussed applying for federal money under various programs. It has been a central part of the Grove's mission to avoid competing for any funds that might otherwise be available to AIDS service organizations (ASOs). By the same token, the Grove has historically been excluded from many funding opportunities that are geared only to ASOs. The Grove's

NAMG STATEMENT OF ACTIVITY FOR YEAR ENDED 12/98

Support and Revenue:	
Hardscape features	$40,169
Planted areas	$145,000
Benches and boulders	$62,633
Circle of Friends	$213,335
Investment income	$96,191
Other revenues	$69,821
Change in pledges receivable	($25,143)
Total support and revenue	**$602,036**
Expenses:	
Wages and benefits	$149,790
Fundraising	$82,382
Education/outreach	$30,883
Other expenses and overhead	$91,627
Total expenses	**$354,682**

designation as a national memorial may ease the situation by making it eligible for funds dedicated to the development and maintenance of national memorials.

Consistent with its initial plan of dissolving the organizational structure when financial goals were reached, the Grove has not yet secured an independent nonprofit status. At the April retreat, however, it was decided to go the nonprofit route after all. In the meantime the Tides Foundation will remain the fiscal agent for the NAMG.

To Name or Not to Name?

The central controversy in the development of the Grove has been the creation of "naming opportunities" for fundraising purposes. Initially, names were intended to appear only in the Circle of Friends, a circular limestone plaza near the east entrance to the Grove. In the Circle, names could be inscribed for a donation of

Memorial benches are simple wood and stone constructions.

$1,000 and represented not only those who had died of AIDS, but other individuals who donated to the Grove in recognition of the crisis. The Circle of Friends has space for 2,200 names. Nine hundred and nine names are currently either inscribed or committed, including such well-known people as Tom Hanks, Elton John, Ryan White, Robin Williams, and Dianne Feinstein.

When Weyand joined the Board in late 1997 he felt strongly, based on his experience with the AIDS Memorial Quilt and other related efforts, that additional giving opportunities – particularly in the range of $5,000 to $25,000 – must be provided to achieve the campaign goals outlined by the Board. Many people initially opposed the idea. They felt that prominently featuring additional donor names would erode the inclusiveness of the Grove and elevate those with the means to provide major donations. Despite resistance from some Board members, in the end the argument to provide naming opportunities was persuasive, and the new campaigns are now well underway. The NAMG brochure offers naming opportunities from $1,000 to $200,000 in such locations as the Fern Grotto ($200,000), South Portal ($100,000), and Redwood Grove ($35,000).

The Bruner Selection Committee felt that the naming controversy was a particularly difficult one: if the names weren't subtle, the Grove might feel like a cemetery, and it might seem inappropriate to single out an economically defined group for memorialization. If, on the other hand, the names appeared *too* subtly, their purpose might not be clear in the future. If a significant central monument were to be constructed, this dilemma would be even more intense – should names go on such a monument? If so, whose? The Committee was sympathetic to the dilemma of the need for fundraising opportunities, but expressed concern about the impact of these fundraising approaches on the Grove.

Large boulder memorial.

PUBLIC AND PRIVATE PARTNERSHIPS

"This public-private partnership has been exemplary in that the objectives of the Recreation and Park Department, i.e., restoring and maintaining an area of Golden Gate Park, have been upheld and merged with the objectives of the Grove in creating an area of peace and reflection honoring those who have lost their lives to AIDS,"
Deborah Learner, Park Planner

Dogwood Crescent boulder memorial

The City of San Francisco

In 1994, in an unusual private-public partnership, the Grove entered into an agreement with the City and County of San Francisco, acting through the Recreation and Park Department. The agreement provides for the Grove to arrange for and to fund site improvements, and to make annual payments to Golden Gate Park for a gardener salary. It requires Golden Gate Park to lease the property to the Grove for a period of 99 years; to maintain the Dell in good condition through a work program subject to annual review; to identify the site as the National AIDS Memorial Grove on signs and maps; and to permit the area to be used for purposes consistent with its dedication, including the ongoing involvement of volunteers.

In addition, the design underwent a lengthy approval process that included reviews by the Site Committee of the Grove Board of Directors, the San Francisco Recreation and Park Department, and the Board of Supervisors. The designers all agreed that the approval process provided a valuable reality check for their work, as it introduced important practical operational considerations. The central elements of the design, however, remained intact throughout the approval process, thanks in no small part to the harmony between Grove's goal of subtlety and the Golden Gate Park's own understated simplicity.

The only ambiguity in the agreement pertains to the acreage involved. The agreement defines the site through a photographic attachment, which was variously described to the Bruner Foundation as a 15-acre and a 7.5-acre site. For practical purposes, the useful area of the Grove is about 7.5 acres. However, Grove designers and management have incorporated some edge areas into their work to ensure the availability of attractive entries into the Grove as well as a seamless border with the Park.

Overall, the City has been pleased with how the Grove has developed. At the most basic level, the expected friction between municipal union gardeners and volunteers has not appeared; indeed, the power of the Grove has been such that a number of City employees actually come to workdays, or even rearrange their schedules so that they can participate in or help out with activities in the memorial. This kind of support can also be found at the political level, where Supervisor Mark Leno is a close ally. Leno was active in the Grove before he was elected to the Board of Supervisors, and continues to be an enthusiastic supporter. Like many others, he came to the Grove to remember a loved one; his partner of 10 years died of AIDS and is memorialized in the Circle of Friends. He took part in early formative discussions about the Grove and has served as a workday volunteer on many occasions. As he stated simply to the site visit team, “If I’m in the Park, I’m in the Grove.”

Concept sketch for the Dogwood Crescent

Concept sketch for Pine Crescent

Golden Gate Park

Golden Gate Park planner Deborah Learner admitted that Park officials needed some convincing in the beginning, as they regularly receive requests for special memorials of different kinds, and promises of maintenance and upkeep have largely gone unfulfilled. In addition, the Park staff was cautious about the presence of large donors, who often want to control the space with which they are associated. Moreover, large donations have historically led to concomitant reductions in General Fund allocations to the Park. These issues, the site visit team noted, are still to a certain extent unresolved: for example, if Park funding is cut, the gardener endowment could be used as an excuse to cut funding to the Park as a whole. Nonetheless, the goal of rehabilitating a truly derelict section of the park, and the powerful cause served by the Grove, convinced the Park that the benefits outweighed the risks.

Ms. Learner expressed concern that volunteers have planted areas that are technically beyond the original boundaries, adjacent to the east entrance; she felt that the gardener position and endowment work should be resolved before acreage is added to the Grove.

The Federal Government

> *One of the vital roles that the Grove serves is as a touch-stone for the grieving process. This is important not only for those of us who have lost loved ones to AIDS, but for everybody; we all have been touched by loss.*
>
> Dianne Feinstein, US Senator

Congresswoman Nancy Pelosi

Nancy Pelosi, a San Francisco native, represents the 575,000 people of the 8th Congressional District. This population was particularly hard hit by AIDS in the late 1980s, when it lost more than 15,000 people to the epidemic, as she puts it, "one person at a time." Many of Representative Pelosi's personal friends died, and many more remain HIV-positive. In part because of her personal involvement in the cause, she has been an active supporter of the Grove: she was an early volunteer, played a role in forging the agreement with Golden Gate Park, and was instrumental in attaining the Grove's national designation. With a busy schedule in Washington, Pelosi continues to participate in workdays about twice a year, and her daughter, an attorney who works with her, now serves on the Board of Directors.

Rep. Pelosi's involvement with the Grove is part of her larger commitment to AIDS issues in Congress. Hers is the lead office in the House of Representatives for AIDS advocacy, she is a vocal advocate for AIDS funding on the House Appropriations Committee, and she is also sponsoring the first housing bill for people with AIDS. While the seriousness and importance of funding for AIDS research is clear to many, she reports, it continues to be an ongoing fight at the congressional level. Partly to help further this larger AIDS battle, Pelosi felt strongly that the Grove should be a national memorial. In the end the national designation was appended to other legislation she was sponsoring relating to the disposition of the Presidio in San Francisco. Passed in 1996, the legislation and the national designation means that the Grove will be included in federal directories of national monuments, and will likely continue to gain stature as a national destination for visitors. The designation brings with it other high honors; as Rep. Pelosi pointed out, First Lady Hillary Rodham Clinton, who visited the Grove in 1998, would probably not have come without the national designation.

FUTURE PLANS

Consistent with the feasibility study prepared for the Ensure Remembrance campaign, immediate plans hinge on increasing the visibility of the Grove on both a local and national level. New Board members Gina Gatta and Len Weise have been selected particularly for their expertise in marketing, and are eagerly making plans for events and relationships that will further this goal. Weise got involved through participation in a twilight donor appreciation event and was "awestruck" by the place. He commented to us, "The Grove is the best-kept secret in San Francisco."

Together Gatta and Weise have forged a marketing and communications plan whose overall objective is "to increase visitation and utilization of the Grove by as broad a constituency as possible." They want the Grove to be used year-round as a venue for AIDS-related events planned once or twice each month. Their strategy is to collaborate with AIDS-related and other organizations; local, state and federal elected officials; and others to promote use of the Grove for educational activities and announcements. Other groups they have targeted, beginning in the Bay Area and ultimately moving to a national basis, include healthcare, education, environmental, arts, and religious organizations. They have also recorded a major public service announcement by actor Tom Hanks, who has been a supporter of the Grove. It was to be aired in major television markets in late 1999.

Several major events are slated to become annual affairs, including the recent highly successful World AIDS Day (December 1) and Arbor Day. The Grove welcomes various uses of this kind, and was pleased when Mayor Brown brought a contingent from the US Conference of Mayors to the Grove in June 1997. Longer-term plans are less clear. The original goal of disbanding when the endowment is secure is very much in question. Newer Board members see a need for an ongoing organization to oversee the maintenance of the Grove, to continue the tradition of workdays, which have become an important programmatic element in the community, and to continue to organize major events that call attention to the AIDS struggle.

A Board retreat in April 1999 addressed mission and purpose, reviewed strategies for soliciting gifts to meet the 2000 endowment goal, and discussed the future of the Grove – what Board members want it to be and what organizational structure is required to achieve that goal. Out of this retreat the Long Range Vision committee was formed.

ASSESSING PROJECT SUCCESS

HOW WELL PROJECT MEETS ITS OWN GOALS

- *To create a living memorial to those whose lives have been affected by AIDS, and a new paradigm for remembrance and renewal.*

Certainly the Grove is a memorial to those who have been affected by AIDS. It is tranquil and welcoming, and provides a metaphorical journey through its woodlands, meadow, and groves. As the first national memorial of its kind, it will increasingly be visited by people from around the country and will doubtlessly inspire similar places throughout the nation. The long-term impact of the place remains to be seen, as it has only recently been completed.

- *To memorialize the scale of devastation wrought by AIDS in San Francisco, an epicenter of the AIDS epidemic, and to raise awareness of the ongoing crisis.*

The nature of the Grove, the design, the Circle of Friends, and other memorial aspects of the Grove are powerful reminders of the tragic losses suffered in the community. The Selection Committee, like some Grove Board Members, noted that the memorial lacks a more dramatic statement or marker that would be a stronger physical evocation of the magnitude of loss. The Board discussed this issue at its most recent retreat.

Other ongoing activities will continue to call attention to the AIDS crisis. Use of the Grove by organizations, especially for public events and announcements, is now actively being solicited. A new public service announcement featuring Tom Hanks will receive national promotion. The Board will continue to focus on increasing visibility of the Grove.

First Lady Hillary Clinton visits the Grove—a new National Memorial

Despite these successes, the Selection Committee felt that the Grove does not yet live up to its billing as a national memorial. While it may be too much to ask that every memorial achieve the power of the Vietnam War Memorial, national status does invite such comparisons, and the Committee felt that some design weaknesses and the lack of a central monument lessened the power of the Grove and kept it from truly measuring up to the level of other national memorials.

- *To create a public place where those who have lost friends or family, those currently afflicted with AIDS, or others can reflect and remember in solitude or can make connections with others.*

The Grove in general, and the workdays in particular, have more than accomplished this goal. The nature of the space allows for individual or collective experiences, and the workdays have been highly successful at helping people make connections they would otherwise not have the opportunity to make. During the site visit team's stay they saw people pausing at the Circle of Friends, and others who were using the Grove as a recreational destination. The Selection Committee affirmed the Grove's quality as a living memorial, a place that seemed to say, "don't feel sorry for me, take action!" This distinguished the site from a cemetery, and also emphasized the importance of process in memorializing and remembering loss.

- *To transform a derelict, 7.5-acre park site into a botanical highlight using an innovative public-private partnership between the City of San Francisco and the nonprofit National AIDS Memorial Grove.*

The Grove appears to have been highly successful in this endeavor. Once an overgrown and dangerous corner of the park, it has been cleared, drained, replanted, and re-designed as a memorial space. Entrances to the Grove are well marked, and invite entry. Good visibility from the street above and from both entries contribute to its inviting aspect and to its safety. Although the memorial spaces are spread throughout the Grove, they do not dominate the experience of moving through it.

From what is known by the site team and the applicants, the design and scale of the Grove are unique in the country if not in the world. Although other communities have inquired about creating similar memorials in their communities, few venues compare to San Francisco in terms of its role in the epidemic and to Golden Gate Park as a nationally known destination. The national designation can only add to the park's ability to attract national constituencies.

- *To develop a vehicle to generate ongoing community stewardship of the Grove and to fund its maintenance in perpetuity.*

This aspect of the Grove is nearly complete. The agreement with the Park secures the site for 99 years with an option to renew the lease. The endowment campaign, which shows every sign of reaching its goals by 2000, will provide for care and maintenance on a permanent basis.

OTHER MEASURES OF SUCCESS

Impact

The impact of involvement on individual participants is undeniable; everyone the site visit team spoke to gave powerful and moving personal testimonials about the effect the Grove had had on their lives. Reportedly, the Grove is visited by a variety of residents and visitors, especially in the summer tourist months. Since the Board does not keep statistics on the number of visitors, it is difficult to tell how many have been touched by it. It is safe to say, however, that as a national memorial with a growing reputation, it will continue to attract more people.

The Grove's newsletter currently reaches about 14,000 people, and the number is growing. In addition, the Grove has put together a "how-to" guide in response to the numerous requests it receives from across the country for tips on how to create similar memorials in other communities. Deborah Learner also reports a constant stream of requests for information about what many consider to be a model of site-specific stewardship in parks. In the best case, the key ideas of the Grove will be adapted to a variety of different settings, and not simply replicated. This kind of adaptation would be the best testimonial to the impact the Grove experience has on visitors.

Finally, the Grove's workdays have fostered strong community building and educational experiences. As described above, the kinds of personal experiences attributed to the workdays by survivors, those who are HIV-positive, youth who had little experience with AIDS, and people who represent different ethnic and racial segments of the community all attest to an important social function being served.

Values Reflected in Development Process

> *"Just getting it built is not the only reason to do something: the festival of creating the Grove is part of the reason for the place."*
> Ira Kurlander, Board member

The central value embodied in the Grove's development is the importance of process. In gathering together, organizing, and working towards a meaningful goal, San Franciscans whose lives have been touched by AIDS have strengthened – and in some cases, created – community ties, performed needed ceremonies of healing and remembrance, and educated others about AIDS-related issues. That these actions can be considered a memorial in themselves, independent of the place they produce, is a provocative statement not only about memorials but about placemaking in general.

At the same time, however, some of the most important values relate very concretely to notions of place. One key lesson the Grove has to teach, for example, is (in the words of Clare Cooper Marcus), that "people care for places that they take care of." In other words, while the workdays might be both inexpensive labor and a living memorial, they are also activities that bind people to the Grove itself, teaching them to care for and about it through active involvement.

A second value embodied in the workdays is their power to draw people across social, ethnic, and racial boundaries. As Elaine Shen remarked, "Working on a place can be a great mediator of difference." As people learn to care about their places, they may also learn to care about each other. While it may seem obvious, there are profound lessons to be drawn from the simple fact that a *place* can be the basis for, or even the generator of, a community. The Selection Committee affirmed that the Grove was a fine example of placemaking, where people's active participation fosters new dialogues and community ties. One site visit team member, remarking on how the Grove literally constructs social relationships, felt the strong pull of the community herself: the park, she explained, "teaches us that we all have AIDS and we all have work to do."

Young volunteers at the close of a workday

FOR FURTHER INFORMATION

Jane Turner Hart, ***Innovations in park and open space stewardship: Case studies and examples in urban park and open space management,*** **(San Francisco: The Trust for Public Land, 1996).** *The first chapter of this book focuses on NAMG, describing the project's background, surveying the volunteer ethic, identifying key design elements, analyzing the structure of the public-private agreement between San Francisco and the NAMG group, sorting through the project's legal and political resources, and investigating funding. It also includes drawings and design sketches.*

Notes From the Grove **[newsletter].** *This quarterly serial presents Grove events and donors.*

Harriet Heyman, "A healing landscape: SF designers honor people with AIDS," ***Garden Design*** **(August / September 1998).** *Interviews with key individuals, lovely color photographs, and a description of the Grove.*

Related Rudy Bruner Award Winners

(For full bibliographic cites, please see Introduction)

Harlem Meer Restoration, New York, New York (1995 cycle). Although not a memorial, this Finalist resembles the Grove in that a nonprofit organization and volunteer labor restored 17 neglected acres in northeast Central Park.

The Stowe Recreation Path (1989 cycle). A blacktop path winding through eleven bridges and 5.3 miles of community back yard. Maintained by volunteers and used widely by residents and tourists.

Contact

National AIDS Memorial Grove
856 Stanyan Street, San Francisco, CA 94117
Telephone: 415-750-8340, Toll-free: 888-29-GROVE
Fax: 415-750-0214
http://www.aidsmemorial.org

Thom Weyand, Executive Director
415-750-8345, thomnamg@aol.com

Trey DeGrassi, Program Manager
415-750-8346, treyde@aol.com

Sueann Mark, Office Manager
415-750-8340, aidsmemgrv@aol.com

The National AIDS Memorial Grove is located near the eastern end of San Francisco's Golden Gate Park at the corner of Middle Drive East and Bowling Green, across from the tennis courts and just east of the California Academy of Sciences.

RUDY BRUNER AWARD FOR URBAN EXCELLENCE

BRUNER FOUNDATION
130 Prospect Street
Cambridge, MA 02139
PH: 617.492.8404
FX: 617.876.4002
www.brunerfoundation.org

1999 Rudy Bruner Award

SILVER
medal winner

ARTScorpsLA

Los Angeles, California

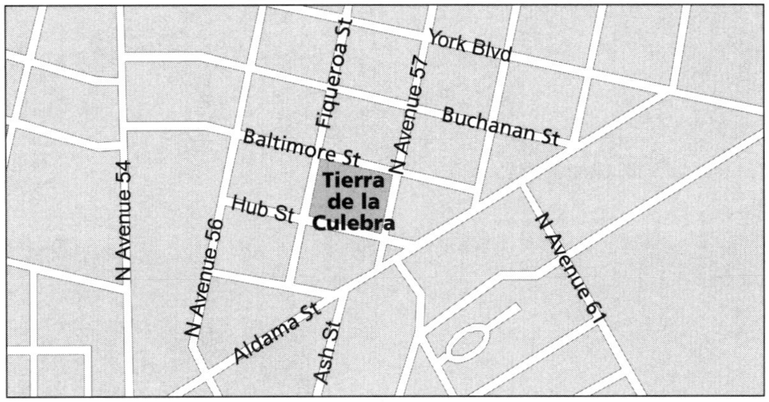
York Blvd
Figueroa St
N Avenue 57
Buchanan St
Baltimore St
Tierra de la Culebra
Hub St
N Avenue 54
N Avenue 56
N Avenue 61
Aldama St
Ash St

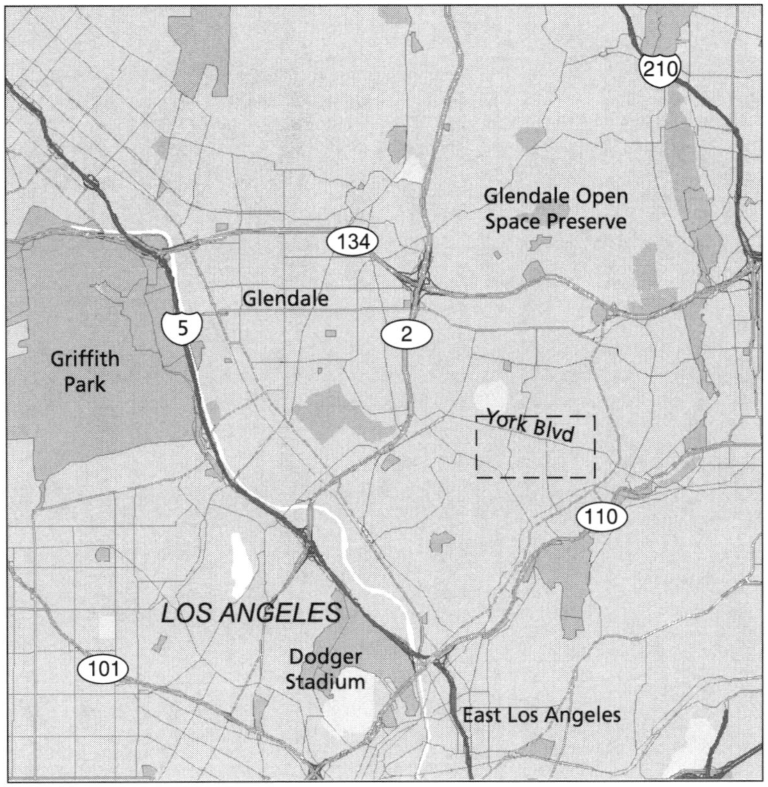
210
Glendale Open Space Preserve
134
Glendale
5
2
Griffith Park
York Blvd
110
LOS ANGELES
101
Dodger Stadium
East Los Angeles

ARTScorpsLA AT A GLANCE

WHO MADE THE SUBMISSION?

- ARTScorpsLA, Tricia Ward, Founder and Director.

WHAT IS ARTSCORPSLA?

- A series of art parks designed, built, and used by local community residents in collaboration with a nonprofit public art and educational organization associated with the University of Southern California.

- Approximately 28 murals throughout the city, created as part of a citywide graffiti abatement program.

- An effort to revitalize local communities in response to the civil unrest of the early 1990s.

- A redefinition of territory, public space, and ownership under the aegis of a private nonprofit organization.

- A training ground and an open cultural and educational space for youth.

- A collaboration among multiple constituencies who have an interest in community open space, arts, education, and youth development.

CHRONOLOGY

1992
Tricia Ward founds ARTScorpsLA and securs an unauthorized garbage dump as the site for the first project, La Tierra de la Culebra.

1995
La Culebra opens.

1995
Spiraling Orchard, another youth-built art park, also initiated on abandoned land in Temple-Beaudry.

1996
ARTScorpsLA takes over abandoned building in Chinatown to develop as office/ studio/ workshop.

1997
ARTScorpsLA asked to assist with Koreatown art park (The Francis Avenue Community Garden).

1994–1999
Walls of Reclamation, a citywide mural project, initiated at the request of the County Open Space & Parks District as part of a graffiti abatement program.

KEY PARTICIPANTS

Individuals who were interviewed are marked with an asterisk [*]

ARTScorpsLA

*Tricia Ward, Founder and Director, ARTScorpsLA

City of Los Angeles

Commission for Children, Youth, and Their Families

*Olivia Mitchell, Assistant Director
*Anne Broussard, Director of Child Care

Councilmember (1st District) Mike Hernandez and his staff:

*Eduardo Reyes, Chief of Staff
*Edward Rodriguez, Chief Planning Director
*David Marquez, Chief Deputy of Legislation and Policy
*Michael Lee, Senior Field Deputy
*Karen Lee, Chinatown Field Deputy

Cultural Affairs Department

*Carla Fantozzi, now Education Manager Museum of Television and Radio.

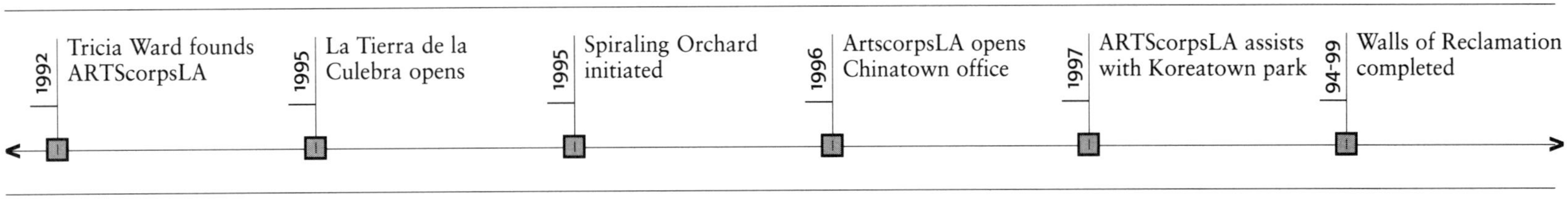

Metropolitan Transportation Authority

*Alan Nakagawa, Senior Public Arts Officer; former member of ARTScorpsLA's board

Architects/Designers

*John Maroney, Tricia Ward
*Roger Hong, AIA, architect

Funding Agencies

ARCO
California Arts Council
*Cheryl Mendoza, Senior Program Officer, California Community Foundation
Cal-Trans Mitigation
Federal Summer Youth Employment
*Karen Lewis, Chair of Philanthropy, Footlighters Foundation
*Nancy Grey, Director, Foundation for the Arts in the Environment
*Gwen Walden, Progam Manager, Getty Trust Fund: Multicultural Intern Program
*Josephine Ramirez, Project Associate, Local and Comparative Research, Getty Research Institute for the History of Art and the Humanities
*Elva Lima, GTE Foundation, Downtown Commission
Los Angeles General Services Department and City Council
Los Angeles Community Redevelopment and Community Development Agencies
Los Angeles Shares
Los Angeles Conservation Corps
Los Angeles County Commission on the Arts
National Service/AmeriCorps
NEA
Sears Foundation
Urban Resources Partnership
Youth Arts and Cultural Affairs Department

Cooperating Organizations

*Bruce Saito, Executive Director, Los Angeles Conservation Corps' Clean & Green Program
Los Angeles Unified School District
Building Up Los Angeles /National Service Commission/ AmeriCorps
Eureka Communities/Fellow
Los Angeles Alliance for a Drug Free Community

VOLUNTEERS AND INTERNS

Aaron Zaima, USC student, volunteer, employee, and Getty intern
*Julie Bach, Jamie Kim, Regan Duffy, current interns
Claudia McDonnell, Public Art Studies graduate student at USC, volunteer
*Margaret Garcia, artist who taught at la Culebra

Community Participants

*Cindy Medina-Diama, local resident
Sal Oseguero, original volunteer, later co-director of Youth Leadership Council (an institutional body of ARTScorpsLA)
*Jaime ("Vyal") Reyes, mural and spray-can artist.
Professional consultant
*Margaret Crawford, Professor of Urban Studies and Theory at Southern California Institute of Architecture (SCIARC)

Others

Carol Goldstein, Professor of Cultural Planning, UCLA
*Inmo, Chinatown Gallery Owner
*Karen Mack, Program Director, Community Partners

PROJECT DESCRIPTION

HISTORY

La Culebra

In 1992, in the wake of civil unrest and violence following the first Rodney King police trial, Los Angeles searched for ways to heal and find reconciliation among its communities. While the business community focused on coordinating philanthropic and grant money through the quasi-public program Rebuild LA, the arts community assisted the Los Angeles Arts Commission in raising money through "Re-Wing LA" (as in helping the City of Angels to once again take flight). Like so many post-riot interventions, these efforts were seen largely as one-shot workshops where artists came into the community, did a project with local residents, and left.

Tricia Ward participated in Re-Wing LA, but was dissatisfied with the "quick-fix" vision it embodied. A veteran of the politically active New York City "Green Guerrillas" and Roosevelt Park Seniors Coalition, she rejected the idea that communities needed "healing," a prescription she described as patronizing and naïve. Rather, she felt, the recent outbreaks of violence had been about the community's lack of voice. True healing could only be the result of democracy, of communities gaining a voice and taking control of their neighborhoods.

Guided by this belief, Ward disengaged herself from Re-Wing LA and initiated a separate project, what would later become La Tierra de la Culebra (the land of the serpent). In both New York and LA, Ward's art had been focused on the use of fallow land; for la Culebra she continued to follow her strengths. Identifying a derelict parcel in her Highland Park neighborhood (east of downtown), Ward gathered young artists from within the immediate neighborhood and began to work with them to clean up the trash that littered the land. This activity began before any permission had been obtained from the owner, but a 9-month use agreement was soon negotiated.

Ward quickly mobilized a group of about 35 youth volunteers to help her transform a site that was, in her words, "a ruin." She felt that the transformation would be most effective if hinged upon a powerful image or symbol. However, she did not select it by herself, as the more typical public artist might. Rather, Ward challenged the youth to find a symbol to represent all the area's cultures (especially Latino, Asian, and white — few African Americans were in the area) and to be positive and forward looking. She held a series of discussions with the young people, who researched symbols and their meanings, finally agreeing on the Mayan and Asian symbol of the serpent (la Culebra).

The Selection Committee was initially concerned about overtones of cultural appropriation in this act, but these concerns were eased once it became clear that the locals themselves chose the symbol based on interpretations of each cultural heritage. In the symbolic

The La Culebra sculpture is made of found objects from the site, mainly river stones and colorful broken tiles.

economy of the Shoshone tribe (upon whose former lands the site rests), the serpent's head signified knowledge, the body growth and movement, and the tail wisdom. Alternative and equally powerful symbolism was found in the myths of the Aztecs and the Asian cultures. While the accuracy of the appropriation of this symbol can be contested, the fact that the Asian and Latino participants found meanings of value to them is not in question. Interestingly, though the serpent was not a viper, some Christians initially took offense. Although some tension still remains, most friction has since dissipated.

Within six months, the site was cleared and the serpent was constructed out of stone at a very low cost, essentially for materials only. Even materials were inexpensive – the bulk of the stone, for example, came from a dry river bed running through the site. At the winter solstice in December of 1992, an Aztec ceremony with dancing and chanting was held to celebrate and consecrate the new park. An amazing 2,000 people participated. During the same winter, ARTScorpsLA formalized itself, attaining the nonprofit (501 C-3) status that enabled them to receive funds for ongoing activity on the site. Since then ARTScorpsLA has, with volunteer labor, completed additional landscaping and other improvements. There are places to walk and sit, hold classes, and give performances. Several murals line the walls, many of which are periodically recreated (as was happening during our site visit). Trees have grown, there is shade, and the site is much more attractive than before.

The la Culebra Property

Over its 7-year history, ARTScorpsLA's relationship with the property owner has been complex. The project started during a real estate slump and, while the landlord intended to build multi-family housing on the site (per its zoning), nothing was likely to happen soon — especially since he was reportedly trying to build at several times the allowable density. However, he does not appear to have managed his ownership or development plans very effectively. In the last two years, he defaulted on one of the four lots that makes up the property, and the bank transferred ownership to ARTScorpsLA. More recently, according to the district's city council representative, the city has formed concrete plans to use available funds to buy the other three lots (for $180,000). They would be owned by the city parks department, but operated by ARTScorpsLA under a lease agreement. Money for improvements such as lighting and fencing would also be available, and ARTScorpsLA is seeking donations for other improvements such as a building with storage space and restrooms. However, the landlord appears to be resisting the city's efforts (possibly to gain leverage in price negotiations). He recently served ARTScorpsLA with an eviction notice, which they are fighting in court. Thus, the long term use of the site by ARTScorpsLA — and its retention as community open space — though probable, is not yet assured.

Spiraling Orchard

With the proven success at la Culebra, ARTScorpsLA began to initiate other community art projects. The other major place-based effort is the Spiraling Orchard, located in a transitional neighborhood called Temple-Beaudry just west and north of downtown, with skyscrapers visible in the background. This parcel is owned by the school district, which acquired it along with a large site nearby where a new high school will be built. It had earlier been part of a site assembled for a Japanese financial center, but a declining real estate market killed the original owner's plans. This particular parcel, discontinuous and too small for school use, was identified by ARTScorpsLA as having positive potential for its community.

In 1995, ARTScorpsLA began to work with the neighbors, this time distributing through the local elementary school a survey designed to help identify the kinds of programs and services needed by the community. The local elementary school distributed the surveys, and they received 250 responses carrying the strong message that after-school programs in the arts were of great need. Ward responded by developing volunteer-based, 10-week 60-kid programs at Spiraling Orchard, designed to include every single family that responded to the survey. The space that developed from this effort is an outdoor park whose centerpiece is a spiral pathway, reinforced by the planting of young trees. In addition, a semi-circular seating area with benches covered in mosaics was created by neighborhood children. Although this site does not revolve around a single cultural symbol like la Culebra, it still strives to be the focus of community activity, both through the youth-oriented programming and through cultural festivals like the one in full swing during the site visit. The site visit team witnessed Aztec troupe chanting and dancing, Spanish-language speeches addressing the meaning of the spiral form, a Mexican-style barbecue, arts and crafts for the kids, and a soccer game. Many neighborhood families appeared to be participating.

Other Projects

Other ARTScorpsLA projects include a large number of murals in various locations (at least 28 are reported to be still in existence), and aid to schools and churches in Koreatown with planning and implementing the Francis Avenue Garden (with much more space devoted to gardening than to art). During our site visit – a sunny Sunday afternoon – the garden's gate was locked, and Ward explained to the site visit team that the whole question of whether there should be a gate had been hotly contested. She had not supported the faction that insisted on its inclusion, but had accepted the decision (and she did have the key).

In addition, in 1996 ARTScorpsLA acquired an office/studio in the old part of Chinatown, and it is expanding to have workshop space there. The new space is centrally located between the two art parks and provides a new set of challenges in terms of working with Chinese residents, who are not always receptive to Anglo or outsider intervention. However, it was reported that ARTScorpsLA has, in the short time it has been there, made some positive impressions and connections, possibly playing a role in attracting a few studios and galleries to the area.

VISION

> *"ARTScorpsLA reveals the link between a healthy environment and healthy humanity through community revitalization projects that incorporate community building, arts and arts education, and the development of life skills."*
> ARTScorpsLA Mission Statement.

At the heart of ARTScorpsLA is the goal of redefining public art. As traditionally conceived, Ward explains, public art would be better described as "plop" art: public money buys something, which is then "plopped" in a public space. ARTScorpsLA has attempted to wrest public art from this artifact-oriented state, where it tends to respond to the dictates of art criticism better than it serves community needs. Ward envisions public art as public process, an ongoing act of creation both grounded in and reinforcing community identity, development, and empowerment. In effect, the arts can be a vehicle for communities to reclaim their urban spaces – "art," as one site visit team member remarked, "as social work."

When approached in this way – as process over product – public art becomes collaborative, populist, "everyday," developing its own audiences even as it is created by its audiences. A crucial part of this dynamic is a commitment to organic (or what Josephine Ramirez calls "jazz") design. Instead of beginning with formal goals and plans, ARTScorpsLA approaches a community with an artistic vision of melding community perspectives into an as-yet undefined community artwork. This provides the artistic (and the practical) room for community visions to sort themselves out and to reach the

Mural workers learn by doing in La Tierra de la Culebra Park.

kind of unifying syntheses represented by the serpent-symbol at la Culebra. It encourages a continual evolution of projects, emphasizes community participation, and ultimately provides community ownership: what begins with an artist's vision ultimately becomes a community's artwork. The parks serve as sites for activities and as "repositories of cultural meaning" rather than as places of passive appreciation of an outside artist's vision. The Selection Committee was particularly impressed by how the project helps teach people to care for their places: by actively engaging the parks – making them and then using them – people attain a genuine connection with these urban places.

By applying this new definition of public art to her traditional bailiwick of urban fallow ground, Ward has drawn out the most provocative ramification of her vision: a reworking of the idea of ownership in public space. In addition to the innovation of substituting a flexible private nonprofit organization for an often rigid city park agency, Ward has infused ARTScorpsLA with a truly radical notion of public space as continually contested territory, belonging to no single owner permanently. Since 1992, la Culebra has moved in and out of turf wars between rival street gangs, sometimes serving as neutral space and at other times being appropriated by one or another gang. (At one point, for example, a group of "OGs" – Old Gangsters – took over the park to provide a safe place for their grandchildren.) Ward has remained resolutely neutral during these shifts, refusing to exercise ownership authority over the site, holding true to her vision of "collaboration – for better or worse." In her view, the gangs are part of the community, and as such must play a role in the continual re-creation of the park.

When taken as seriously as it is by Ward, this kind of approach can obviously create both minor and serious problems. ARTScorpsLA has had a problem with theft of books and tools, for example, but Ward smilingly explains that "this is a *good* thing," because it means they are wanted and are being used. Also, there have been some difficulties with the police when a temporarily dominant gang has crossed the boundaries of acceptable behavior in the park. When one such gang began conspicuously drinking in public at the site, for example, the police had to act against them, causing friction between Ward and many locals since she was inaccurately portrayed as the instigator of the busts. The worst incident was the murder of a gang member near the Culebra site. Despite these problems, however – and Ward herself might not even describe all of them as problems – there is no denying the potential power of the collaborate-with-everyone philosophy when trying to create a place that has real meaning for its community.

Supplies are stored in a neighbor's garage immediately adjacent to la Tierra de la Culebra.

Obviously, a key part of ARTScorpsLA's re-negotiations of art and public space is a commitment to openness and collaboration with multiple constituencies. As Ward's collaborative philosophy dictates, no exclusion is practiced – even dedication of a project to its immediate community or neighborhood, if that were to mean excluding others based on class, race, age, ethnicity, or geography. Thus, the participants and programs at a given site could be constantly changing. Clearly, Ward also accepts the fact that inclusion at this level inevitably invites conflict and confrontation. The working out of divergent positions, she maintains, is an essential part of the process, rather than an obstacle to be avoided. Ultimately, this kind of project can provide a voice for people of widely different backgrounds, and can knit them together in a common cause.

Finally, the ARTScorpsLA vision places community at the heart of the artistic process. Beyond providing settings for evolving community relationships, the parks have focused on providing for youth a kind of experiential learning that plays out through a non-hierarchical, self-organizing process. This process can seem unstructured, but is intended to shift responsibility to the learner. Teaching formats include mentoring, various levels of participation, and allowing youth to discover principles themselves – and thus the space and freedom to fail along the way.

ORGANIZATION AND LEADERSHIP

Tricia Ward

The dominant force in ARTScorpsLA is its founder and leader, Tricia Ward, who funded the early activities out of her own pocket and later created the organization as a vehicle to attract and manage funding and to lease or take title to sites. Ward is universally acknowledged both for being highly unusual ("really weird" in the impressed words of one interviewee) and for being unusually open to collaboration with others. One site visit team member noted that "Ward is not inclined to linear thinking," an observation that appears to coincide with her distaste for linear planning and process. In addition to sparking her creativity, this characteristic also may play a part in Ward's most widely praised attribute: her willingness to listen. Olivia Mitchel, the Assistant Executive Director of the LA Commission for Children, Youth, and Their Families described Ward with respect as "a white woman who listens." In Chinatown, Ward gained trust in a community traditionally suspicious of Anglos by having all of her first steps be about paying attention: she asked Chinatown community leaders to walk with her looking at potentially worthwhile properties, and then intervened to stop demolition of a decorative wall that she had observed was central to a local movie being filmed. At an even more committed level, Ward refused to exercise power to shape the way gangs responded to the la Culebra park, instead choosing to value their activities as part of a community process that she had no right to control.

Her unique gift – what might be called a genius for listening – allows Ward to collaborate with an amazingly broad range of people, "from the Gettys to the gangs," as described to the site visit team. As an Anglo, she also appears to be unusually capable of

The artist Tricia Ward, Founder and Director of ARTScorpLA

gaining acceptance by other ethnic groups. She works extensively in mostly Latino neighborhoods, and is City Council Member Mike Hernandez's appointed representative to the city's Commission for Children, Youth, and their Families. As Councilman Hernandez explained, Ward has been accepted not only by Latinos; she has been able to penetrate the very closed culture of Chinatown more effectively than his own Chinese-American aide. The site visit team observed Ward interacting with neighborhood youngsters with a combination of affection and discipline, expressing high expectations for their behavior and accomplishments. They saw her giving encouragement to Latino artists in their teens and twenties, several of whom worked on the projects' murals and who credited Ward with helping them take advantage of important opportunities. They also heard the compliments of staff at a variety of city agencies, community-based organizations, and charitable foundations who were uniformly positive in describing the impacts of her projects and interventions.

The Selection Committee noted that ARTScorpsLA shows signs of being a one-woman show, but there is also evidence that the organization may be growing beyond its dependence on Ward and architect John Maroney. Ward teaches at the University of Southern California, and has brought a significant number of her graduate students to do their practicums through ARTScorpsLA. Some have continued with their projects even after graduating. Many community youths have received scholarships through ARTScorpsLA and have continued to work on its projects. And ARTScorpsLA has been effective in obtaining funding from a very wide variety of sources and in cooperating with many, sometimes casually related, community organizations. Nonetheless, the Selection Committee recognized that at this point Ward remains the solitary central figure. This reflects Ward's dynamism and creativity, but it also suggests the presence of what one interviewee called "founder's disease": despite her commitment to community rather than artist control, Ward has been reluctant to loosen her hold on ARTScorpsLA's reigns. MTA Senior Public Arts Officer Allen Nakagawa explained that he left ARTScorpsLA's Board of Directors because he felt that the organizational structure was inappropriate; what Ward really needed was an Advisory Council.

The Selection Committee also commented on a potential downside to Ward's unique leadership style: can it be sustained? Indeed, is it even *about* permanence to any significant degree? As one interviewee explained, Ward's urban interventions are all about "organizing for 'not-forever.'" This philosophy is in accord with her ideas of non-linearity, collaboration, and public space as contested "turf," but it is not exactly a sturdy basis on which to found a long-term process – it requires, by its nature, constant maintenance, constant creativity, constant attention, and enormous energy, all from someone with the determination and skills of a Tricia Ward. In short, the Committee felt, ARTScorpsLA may not be just a one-woman show; its animating spirit may also depend on the unreplicable creativity of a single individual as well. Another Selection Committee member responded to this observation, however, by suggesting that fragility and impermanence may sometimes be a positive thing.

ARTScorpsLA

ARTScorpsLA's organizational structure is evolving. Owing to its initially very loose structure, there are concerns regarding ongoing management and operation. Several informants referred to a "lack of consistent presence of ARTScorpsLA" at the sites; according to one, "due to a small staff, there have been periods of time where the site has been neglected." Committed to a wide range of functions and outside obligations, Ward may have spread herself too thin.

New organizational structures have been put in place to address some of these issues. For each project, there is now a site leader or developer who has day-to-day responsibility, in theory freeing Ward to focus on policy, planning, and funding – not always an easy transition for a hands-on artist. Also, there are mechanisms at each site for gathering community input and ownership. At la Culebra, there is a Youth Leadership Council which organizes activities and enforces the rules (described by ARTScorpsLA as a "self-governing administrative body") as well as a group of Mothers of Culebra.

ARTScorpsLA continues to study its organizational structure with an eye toward improvement. Ward rejected an initial, academic assessment that suggested a more rigid structure. More recently, however, ARTScorpsLA has received technical assistance from Deb Grotfeldt, executive director of Project Row Houses (a Rudy Bruner Award Silver Medallist in 1997), who recommended more structure and focus for ARTScorpsLA to function at a higher level of efficiency. Key suggestions included hiring an executive or administrative director to free Ward from running daily operations, clarifying the roles of other staff and site managers, and reconstituting the board of directors, adding individuals who could help with policy, fundraising, and networking. Ward agrees with the suggestions, is looking for an executive director, and will be inviting new board members. To a considerable degree, the future success of ARTScorpsLA would seem to depend on the success of these initiatives.

Since the Site Visit, ARTScorpsLA's efforts to develop a new Board of Trustees have made progress. Positions on the Board have already been accepted by an attorney from a large firm, the manager of the Reinvestment Act from Sanwa Bank, and a local developer. A request to the new General Manager of Recreation and Parks for the City of LA is pending. Additional members are still being considered to develop the small new governing body.

DESIGN

The Artparks

La Culebra

The la Culebra site is made up of four rectangular parcels, with a steep slope from street to back and across the middle parcels. The giant snake figure, made of river stones as well as colorful broken tiles and other found artifacts, is one of several devices that integrate the parcels. Another is a path system that works its way through the site, and a third is a series of landscape transitions on the steep slopes. There are two major entries from the street, one on the

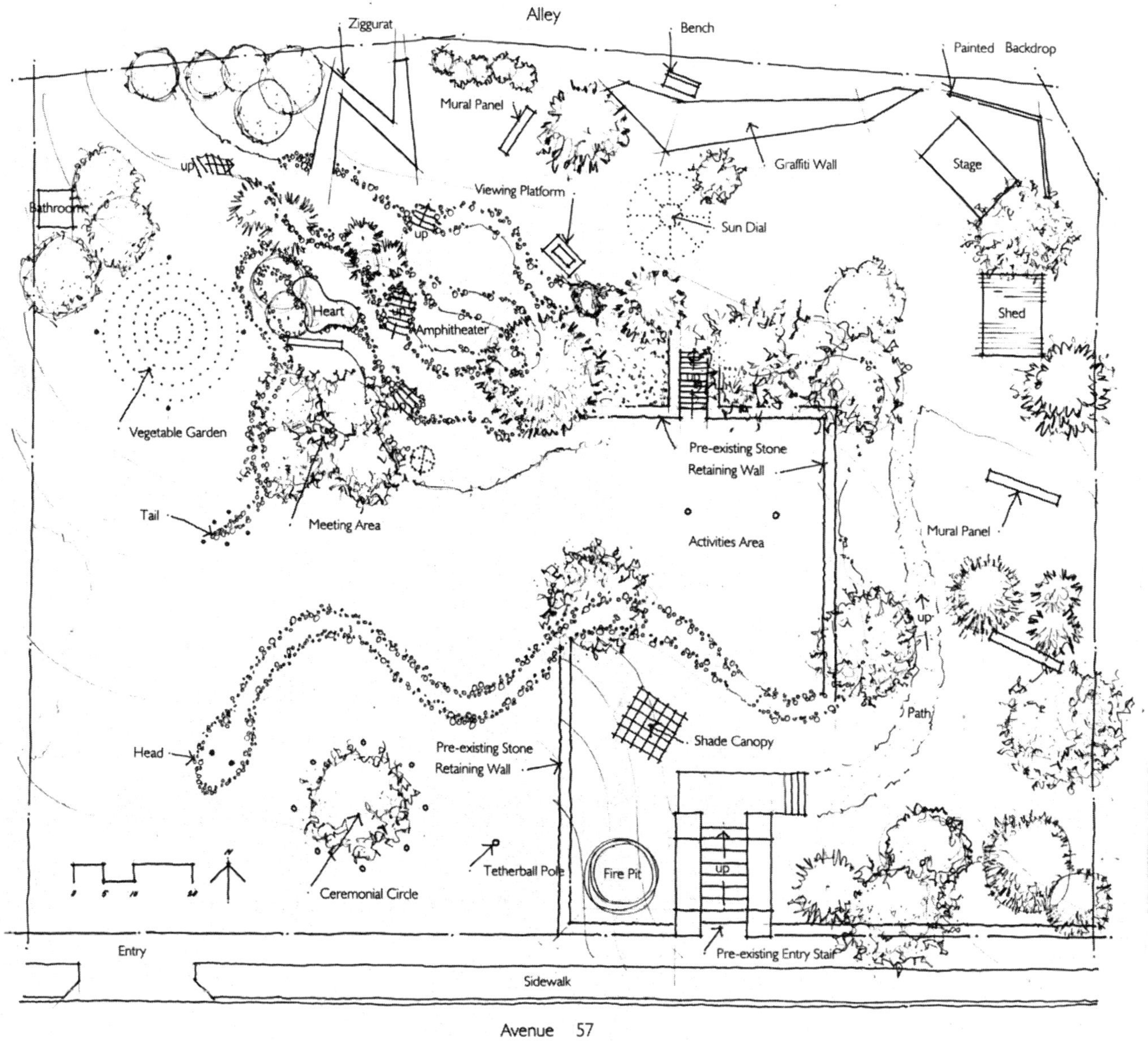

Site Plan drawing describing La Tierra de la Culebra.

lower edge and one through an upper set of stairs. The landscape features have matured such that large, open spaces as well as intimate places can be found. Moving through the park is an act of discovering these places. One site visit team member described it as an "unpretentious landscape plan – not a ton of attention to detail, somewhat organic, but it seems to work."

Spiraling Orchard

The site consists of two lots that slope steeply upward from the street. One has an old oil tank typical of this neighborhood riddled with skeletons of pumping and storage equipment. Children have painted signs and murals on walls and on the tank. The second lot has the "spiraling orchard" toward the top of the slope. The spiral is incised into the earth and planted with small fruit trees (apricots and nectarines) placed every few feet. They will, eventually, be espaliered to form a continuous surface (when in leaf) that one can follow to the center. At this point, the Spiraling Orchard does not have park-like landscape features or site subdivisions in place as does la Culebra, although it does have structural chairs and benches with Culebra-like construction. Some of the public art, for example the old oil tank, is already in place.

Spiraling Orchard opening ceremonies

Steps at ARTScorpsLA's la Tierra de la Culebra feature glass and tile mosaic wok.

Murals

ARTScorpsLA is a prolific producer of public murals, having completed more than 30 of them in the past seven years (28 of which are still reported to be in existence). Generally, young artists have started working at the Culebra and then been given a role on the mural team. It is something of an honor to be part of the mural team, and interns have to demonstrate dedication as well as talent to gain a place. One particularly ambitious mural, "Earth Memories," painted on a retaining wall at Belmont High School, is 600 feet long and tells the story of the evolution of the universe. Others are in various inner-city locations and many have strongly political or cultural themes. The next mural will be around the construction fence at City Hall.

Urban Context

Highland Park and Temple-Beaudry are approximately 80% Latino. Residents live predominantly in multi-family structures, with 2-3 generations sharing an apartment. More than 50% of youth are below the poverty line, the high school dropout rate is higher than 60%, and the unemployment rate is 12% (dates for this information were not available). Councilman Hernandez showed the site visit team maps printed from the city's geographic information system (GIS) that plotted other socio-economic indicators which showed that his district, particularly where ARTScorpsLA is working, has the highest concentration in Los Angeles of factors that indicate poverty and social disintegration. Construction of more than 500 new units of housing in Temple-Beaudry is now underway, which will help to stabilize the area's resident population.

Spiraling Orchard opening ceremonies

ARTScorpLA mural work - one of twenty-eight still in existence on LA buildings.

ARTScorpsLA Programs

Consistent with its mission, ARTScorpsLA offers a variety of activities, mostly arts- and culture-related, some just fun. Some of the activities occur on a regular schedule – especially at la Culebra – principally after school and on Saturdays, since they are youth-oriented. In the months preceding our site visit these included arts and crafts (making dolls, musical instruments, masks, murals, sculpture classes, glassmaking, and so on), poetry workshops, Aztec drumming and dancing, and various sports, as well as festivals celebrating Summer Solstice and Valentines Day.

Other programs are oriented toward job training and employment, and ARTScorpsLA has consistently received funds from AmeriCorps to support these efforts. In these programs, community youth receive a stipend to work on ARTScorpsLA's projects. Teens might begin as volunteers, move on to trainee status (with an honorarium), and then become paid mentors as they demonstrate skills and commitment. Ultimately, they could become site instructors when they have shown an ability to work with younger children.

Teaching is an important part of ARTScorpsLA's mission. It integrates graduate students in public arts with its community projects. Each graduate student plans a project that might last for a day, a week or a month and executes it with community participants. Since 1993, the Getty Trust has funded a few internships for ARTScorpsLA to support the students who have demonstrated the greatest commitment and effectiveness. ARTScorpsLA has provided 62 scholarships to youth from the la Culebra neighborhood to pursue higher education. These young people have, in turn, worked with hundreds or thousands of children throughout the greater Los Angeles area.

FINANCING

Total development cost of la Culebra was about $212,000, and the site has an annual operating budget of about $20,000. The project was initially funded with money from Ward's own savings account. The subsequent variety of sources testifies to the creativity and

Picnic and mural at la Tierra de la Culebra

persistence of ARTScorpsLA fundraising (see table). For Spiraling Orchard, the cost so far has been in the range of $ 40,000, with the bulk of it coming from two grants: $20,000 from the NEA Program for Art in Public Places for outreach and original designs, lease, and so forth; and another $12,000 from the LA City Department of Cultural Affairs to pay kids to work on the amphitheater.

With a renewed lease from Los Angeles Unified School District in 1999, ARTScorpsLA has been feverishly applying for funds to sustain the further development of Spiraling Orchard. To date, the S. Mark Taper and Plum Foundations have provided funds for a job training program, BULA/Americorps program has supported scholarships for young people, and Good Works Foundation and Sanwa Bank have helped fund artists/mentors. Additionally, ARTScorpsLA has submitted proposals to the Staples, Robinson, and Stein Foundations, and the NEA.

ARTScorpsLA operates on a cash budget of a little over $200,000 per year, plus in-kind donations of almost another $100,000. Last year's funding sources are shown in the following table. (Note that both cash and in-kind are included on the same list and that some monies flowed directly to participants without going through ARTScorpsLA's books):

1997 FUNDING SOURCES	AMOUNT
ARCO	$10,000
California Arts Council (directly to artists, not ARTScorpsLA)	$7,000
California Community Foundation	$13,000
Footlighters Foundation	$38,000
Getty Multicultural Intern Program	$10,000
Getty Trust Fund	$20,000
GTE	$3,000
LA Community Redevelopment Agency	$50,000
LA Shares (in-kind: supplies)	$20,000
LA Youth Arts and Cultural Affairs Department	$13,000
LA Conservation Corps (plus $4,000 for in-kind volunteers)	$15,000
LA County Commission on the Arts	$4,000
National Service/Americorps ($46K labor, $20K scholarships)	$66,000
Urban Resources Partnership	$25,000
TOTAL	**$294,000**

ARTSCORPSLA AND THE CITY OF LOS ANGELES

The relationship between ARTScorpsLA and the City of LA is a complicated one. ARTScorpsLA was, after all, born out of Tricia Ward's unwillingness to put up with the red tape she encountered in the government-run Re-Wing LA, and she has continued to refuse funding if it is encumbered by "healing" agendas or other unwanted baggage. Nonetheless the City has proven an invaluable ally on the financial ledger (see table in "Financing"), and has also helped ARTScorpsLA in the procurement of sites. Currently, for example, ARTScorpsLA has asked and has been promised eventual ownership of the la Culebra site, and applications are in line to provide city-funded water, fences, and money for maintenance.

If Ward has occasionally been wary of the City, she has nevertheless gained some staunch allies there, including Councilmember Mike Hernandez. Hernandez was very impressed with what Ward has been able to accomplish working in a very tough neighborhood, reminding the site visit team that Jackson Browne's song "Born on the Avenues" was about this area. As he summarized it, she made a park, with no resources, working with the community, on land she didn't own that was not zoned for public open space. Nor was she helped by the widespread prejudice against the youths Ward hoped the park would serve. Hernandez liked the fact that Ward had captured the kids' imaginations and gotten them to visualize what the space could be like through their own creativity. He feels that la Culebra is a model of effective grassroots action, and he likes to take politicians there to see it — to show them how much can be done with limited resources when the peoples' energy is harnessed. He has taken mayoral candidates, the incumbent mayor, state senators, and congressmen to la Culebra. He also goes there to read to the kids and to talk to them. La Culebra, he feels, is a kind of communications bridge, a place where the youth, even the troubled ones, have become stakeholders and treat it as "sacred ground" – neutral turf, free of graffiti, a place where gangs can sign peace treaties.

Other City allies include Allen Nakagawa, who reported to the site visit team that the project has helped to "inspire" the MTA to extend public transportation beyond its present service area, which ends near where the King riots began. As yet, there has been no action on this plan.

FUTURE PLANS

Not including the murals, which are relatively limited in scope, ARTScorpsLA's two main projects are works in progress. La Culebra is a substantial accomplishment, having completely transformed its site and having had enough time for the landscaping to mature. It will continue to evolve, perhaps through a planned support building (the "Footlighter's House of Dreams") with a kitchen, restrooms, library, computers, and second-floor quarters for an artist-in-residence. Spiraling Orchard is far less complete, though much work has been done there, too. The fruit trees will grow, more planting will be done, murals will be added or redone, and more amenities will be installed. In terms of organization and governance, the goal is to make the art parks self-governing community centers by having youth councils and parents' groups make decisions and provide needed management (see "Organization and Leadership").

ARTScorpsLA is currently involved in several other projects, including painting murals at City Hall and assisting a community garden and arts project in Koreatown. They are also in discussion with the LA Conservation Corps about taking responsibility for developing an art park on part of a 20-acre site called Debs Park in East LA. With the same group, ARTScorpsLA is participating in a grant-funded project from the Community Redevelopment Agency to design a new park bench from recycled materials. Another project is proposed to have a reptilian theme ("Reptilia Island"), but will undoubtedly evolve in the usual ARTScorpsLA interactive manner.

Negotiations with the City to establish a public-private partnership are underway and may prove to be the policy precedent that ARTScorpsLA has been working to establish since its inception. This undertaking is linked to the acquisition of the la Culebra land and a number of improvements, such as designing and building a sculptural fence around the perimeter of the park; lighting and irrigation systems; and securing all masonry walls and the sculptural Culebra for the future. Construction on the Footlighter's House of Dreams will begin when the partnership with the City has been negotiated, which is projected to be during winter 2000. This partnership will also determine the premise for development of Reptilia Island and the Renaissance Skill Center in Debs Park.

ASSESSING PROJECT SUCCESS

HOW WELL PROJECT MEETS ITS OWN GOALS

- *To have a long-term impact on the quality of life by facilitating highly innovative uses of land.*

It is too early to judge the long-term impact of a project that started seven years ago and is still evolving. However, both of the sites entail innovative land use and have positively affected the quality of life for people in their immediate area.

- *To foster direct short- and long-term community involvement, sense of ownership, empowerment, and commitment/pride.*

Members of the community at each site have been involved in its creation and participate in its activities. A good number of people did express a sense of ownership, community self-awareness, and pride to the site visit team.

- *To develop creativity, environmental awareness, interpersonal leadership, and trade skills that will prepare local teens for paid jobs.*

Although no tracking data are available, many observers and participants spoke of the growth they had seen or experienced through working on ARTScorpsLA projects. Graduate students were having valuable experiences working on community art, children were learning art and cultural skills, and teens were working on construction and art projects that have led to paid employment, not only with ARTScorpsLA but also on commercial and other public art projects.

- *To strengthen family ties and community cultural self-esteem.*

In Cindy Medina-Dima's family the site visit team saw one example of strengthened family ties, and the team also observed participation in cultural activities, such as the Aztec ceremony at Spiraling Orchard, and were shown the importance of the cultural symbols incorporated into artworks. Apparently, these symbols (including the serpent), especially once they are consecrated, are meaningful to a broad range of community members. Even the police thought of la Culebra as sacred ground.

OTHER MEASURES OF SUCCESS

Impact on Neighborhood and Community

According to most people with whom the site visit team talked, ARTScorpsLA's impact has been aesthetic and inspirational. New community organizations have sprung up, youth have been positively engaged, employed, and trained, and there are more places for them to spend their time productively and safely. Local youths interviewed on site praised Ward as a comfortable and open woman, and expressed gratitude for the opportunities ARTScorpsLA offered them. Parents appreciated the safe public space for family outings. As one of the youths described Culebra, many see the parks as a "sanctuary, a gift to the community." These positive experiences have mainly been centered in two neighborhoods.

Gangs and Crime

The areas in which ARTScorpsLA works are considered classic inner-city neighborhoods in terms of their socio-economic profiles. In addition, they are high crime zones, with gang turf conflicts and related struggles over shifting boundaries. In this difficult terrain ARTScorpsLA has tried to provide real solutions – employment, job training, youth mentoring, cultural affirmation – to some of the issues that Ward felt had boiled over in the riots. More fundamentally, the organization has continued to adhere to the challenging model of true collaboration that Ward believes creates a safe zone for the community's voices to be heard. This process is one that will never bring clear, unalloyed success. Continual breakdowns, conflicts, and re-negotiations are built into the script. Thus, while many locals did tell the site visit team that ARTScorpsLA has helped ameliorate living conditions, at least on the territory where they operate directly, the long story of periodically unpleasant gang involvement reveals what Ward would consider a successful but obviously never-finished story.

Place vs. Process – The Crucial Issue

Beyond leadership and sustainability issues, the Selection Committee's primary concerns with ARTScorpsLA were questions about the nature and meaning of urban excellence. The basic question was whether ARTScorpsLA is ultimately a *place* or a *process*. Clearly, there are elements of both in the projects; the parks do exist, after all, and they are explicitly based on a provocative philosophy of process. What the Selection Committee grappled with was where the power and *excellence* of

The Francis Avenue Garden center walkway

ARTScorpsLA really lay: in the parks, or in the process that has created and sustained them?

Most members of the Committee did agree that in this instance the process of generating community involvement and caring about public spaces was more impressive than their physical quality. The parks were interesting but did not warrant an award for design. The radical notions of public art and public space embodied in Ward's design process and in the usage of the parks over time were more innovative than any single public artwork that they produced.

This led some Committee members to ask whether ARTScorpsLA presents a challenge to our notions of place, forcing us to expand them not just in breadth but in depth to include the rituals and practices that create and nurture places. Others felt that, even so, it would still be inappropriate to award the Gold Medal to a project that seemed so overbalanced towards process compared to the actual places that had been created. One Committee member speculated that a consequence of this emphasis on process may be that fewer people are ultimately reached: participation may be a life changing experience for local youths, but only for those youths who actually choose to *participate*. It is not enough to simply experience the place; to be thus affected, one must engage the process as well, and this necessarily limits the constituency.

The Selection Committee concluded that an excellent and innovative process does not necessarily lead to a great space, at least in conventional design terms. At la Culebra, a good place was indeed created, and there is evidence that it continues to benefit from the processes that brought it into being: the cultural festivals, the youth programs, and the shifting patterns of public usage all speak to Culebra being more than just a park. The nature of the Spiraling Orchards is still to be determined. In the best case, it too will institutionalize the welcoming processes that have made Culebra such a meaningful location; in the worst case, it will simply be a pretty, but unremarkable, urban park. Culebra, too, could have such a future in store for it, depending on how well it sustains the rituals and loose structures that make it special. These unresolved issues make ARTScorpsLA an important project to continue watching. To the extent, however, that community building is an important aspect of urban excellence, the ultimate physical form of the parks may be less important than the bridges built among diverse communities.

Questions of place and process also raise the issue of sustainability. Ward's own philosophy of contestation, fluidity, and change – planning for the "not-forever" – left the Selection Committee wondering whether permanence was even a goal of the project. With its organizational challenges and its unique form of tenancy (leasing land from a hostile owner), this is no idle question. The Committee then discussed the importance of sustainability in urban excellence. Is an essentially ephemeral intervention, almost a performance art piece, enough? No firm conclusions were reached on this thorny issue, in part because it is difficult at this early stage of the game to measure ARTScorpsLA's legacy over time. Nonetheless the Committee acknowledged the power of ARTScorpsLA to provocatively raise issues such as this that force us to question the very meanings of the term "urban excellence."

Values Reflected in Development Process

As has become clear, most of this project's power emanates from the values embodied in its development process. The idea of using a redefined concept of public art to positively destabilize public spaces in a way that gives voice to community residents of all stripes, while at the same time providing a ladder of opportunity for those who wish to take it, is clearly the central informing value and the most notable element of the project. Whether such impressive programmatic values can, by themselves, be considered sufficient grounds for the highest accolades of urban excellence, remains an open question – and a question that must, the Selection Committee felt, be counted among this remarkable project's many contributions.

ARTScorpsLA: Teaching life skills through the arts

FOR FURTHER INFORMATION

Dickerson, Amina and Tricia Ward, "A co-meditation on youth, art, and society," in Mary Jane Jacob and Michael Brenson, eds., *Conversations at the Castle* (The MIT PRESS, 1998). *See pp. 150-60 for a section on ARTScorpLA. The full book addresses questions inherent in public arts programs: Who is contemporary public art for?*

Dunitz, Robin J. and James Prigoff, *Painting the Town, Murals of California*, (R.J.D. Enterprises, 1997). *See p. 200 "Earth Memories" on an ARTScorpLA mural. The book profiles 300 murals in 50 California towns.*

Jacob, Mary Jane, Michael Brenson and Eva M. Olson, *Culture in Action: A Public Art Program of Sculpture Chicago*, (Bay Press, Inc., 1995). *A Chicago-based community art program focused on "urban artmaking" related to critical social issues. Like ARTScorpLA, the program pushes the boundaries of public art.*

Related Rudy Bruner Award Winners

(For full bibliographic cites, please see Introduction)

Radial Reuse Plan, Lincoln, Nebraska (1989 cycle). A participatory process that created a 3 mile linear park connecting neighborhoods on land formerly intended to be a major roadway. Sparked neighborhood revitalization in adjacent areas.

Project Row Houses (1997 cycle). Rehabilitation of 22 historic "shotgun" style houses into art galleries showcasing the work of prominent African-American artists, housing and support services for single working mothers, and a variety of daycare and after-school programs.

Contact

ARTScorpsLA
Tricia Ward, Director and Founder
Julie Bach, Coordinator of Creative Projects
936 Mei Ling Way
Los Angeles, CA 90012

Phone: 213-617-3877 or 3876
Fax: 213-617-3878
E-mail: aclaacla@earthlink.net
Web: http://home.lacn.org/lacn//artscorpsla/index.html

RUDY BRUNER AWARD FOR URBAN EXCELLENCE

BRUNER FOUNDATION
130 Prospect Street
Cambridge, MA 02139
PH: 617.492.8404
FX: 617.876.4002

www.brunerfoundation.org

1999 Rudy Bruner Award

SILVER
medal winner

PARKSIDE PRESERVATION
Philadelphia, Pennsylvania

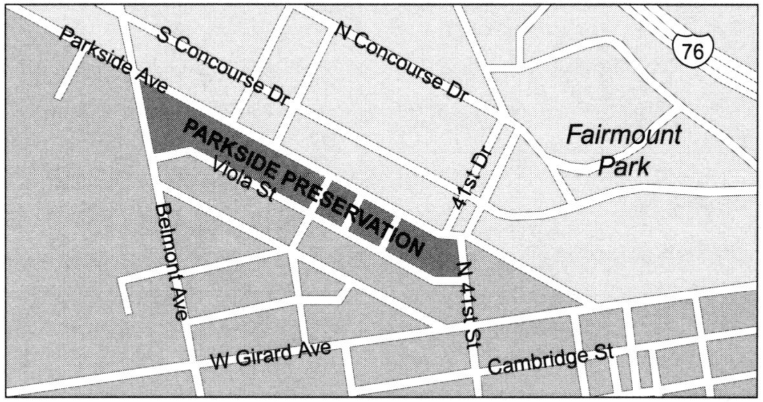
Parkside Ave
S Concourse Dr
N Concourse Dr
76
Fairmount Park
PARKSIDE PRESERVATION
Viola St
41st Dr
Belmont Ave
N 41st St
W Girard Ave
Cambridge St

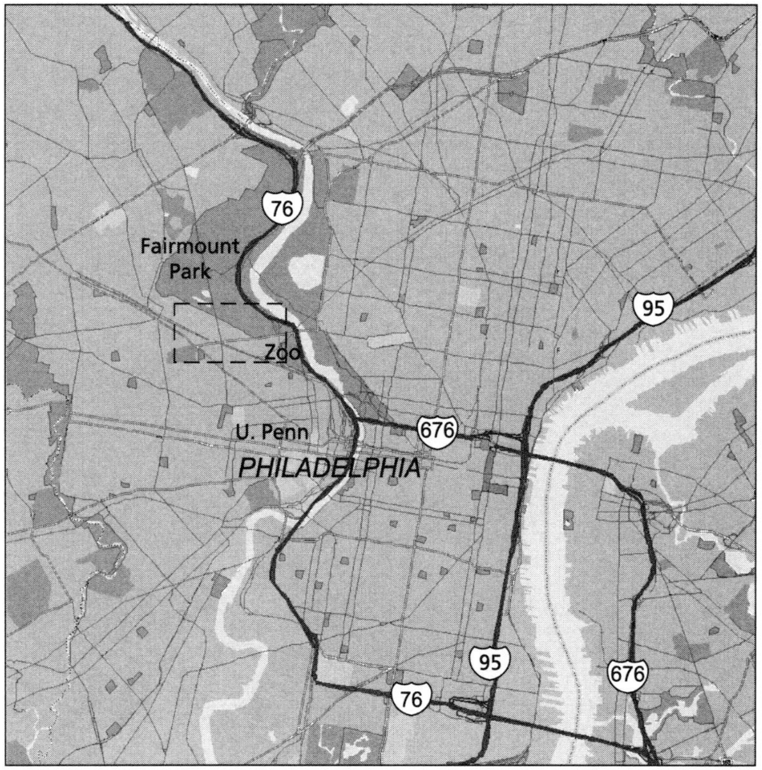
76
Fairmount Park
Zoo
95
U. Penn
676
PHILADELPHIA
95
676
76

PARKSIDE PRESERVATION AT A GLANCE

WHO MADE THE SUBMISSION?

- Parkside Historic Preservation Corporation, James L. Brown, IV, Executive Director.

WHAT IS PARKSIDE PRESERVATION?

- Historic restoration of several blocks of late 19th-century mansions on Parkside Avenue, facing Fairmont Park.

- Revival of portions of a well-defined and tightly bounded neighborhood characterized by poverty, abandonment, and depopulation.

- A mixture of low- and moderate-income housing for working families and groups with special needs, including substance abusing women with children, people with AIDS/HIV, people with mental and physical disabilities, and the elderly.

- An effort to revitalize and capitalize a predominantly African-American neighborhood to preserve significant buildings, and to serve current residents.

CHRONOLOGY

1963
: James Brown IV purchases six-unit building at 4218 Parkside Ave for $12,000 and rehabilitates it.

1967
: Brown and his partners buy 19-unit Landsdowne and form the Parkside Development Corporation. Cosmetic rehabilitation is completed by 1972.

1970s
: Brown and his wife, as private developers, accumulate nine more properties with 45 units on Parkside Ave over next two decades, but bank redlining makes construction difficult.

1982
: Brown asks University of Pennsylvania architectural historian George Thomas to conduct historic district research.

1983
: Parkside Historic Preservation Corporation (PHPC) founded. Parkside Historic District placed on National Register of Historic Places. More thorough and historically correct restoration of Landsdowne is completed.

1993
: Brantwood restoration completed and occupied by Philadelphia Health Management Corporation.

1994
: Pennrose Properties wins RFP for rights to restore Brentwood and partners with Parkside Historic Preservation Corporation.

1996
: Brentwood completed.

1996
: Parkside Historical District Coalition formed with 10 area organizations.

1999
: Brantwood II completed.

1999
: Parkside-Pennrose partnership restores Marlton for "We Are the People with AIDS/HIV."

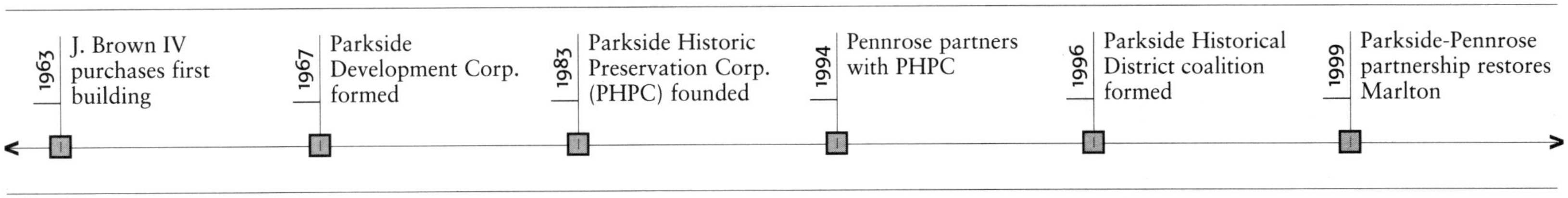

KEY PARTICIPANTS

Individuals who were interviewed are marked with an asterisk [*]

Community Developers

*James Brown IV, Executive Director, Parkside Historic Preservation Corporation
*John Rosenfield and Robert Totaro, Pennrose Properties
*Leonard Goldman, private developer

Parkside Historic District Coalition

*Anthony Venuto, Director, Belmont Housing Corporation, a subsidiary of Inglis House (provides skilled care to people with mobility disabilities)
Bryn Mawr Presbyterian Church (a suburban congregation with a history of commitment to the area and a partnership with First African)
*Pastor Joseph Ginyard, Gospel Chapel (in the area for 36 years, the Chapel has operated a transitional home for homeless women and has adopted the Leidy School)
Christ Community Baptist Church
*Ron Shelton, Executive Director, Habitat for Humanity West Philadelphia (a nonprofit affiliated with Habitat International, which partners with the First African Church to create affordable, owner-occupied housing)
*Pastor Henry L. Pinkney, First African Presbyterian Church (the first African Presbyterian Church in America and Habitat for Humanity's community partner, the church operates several social service programs)
Leidy Elementary School (the only public school in East Parkside, it provides childcare and GED classes for the community)
*Parkside Historic Preservation Corporation
*John Loeb, Vice President, Philadelphia Health Management Corporation (PHMC, a nonprofit public health organization, it provides direct services, program evaluation, and technical support for health care)
*Alexander Hoskins, President/CEO, Philadelphia Zoo
*Walter Kubiak, Executive Director, 1269 Housing Corporation (a nonprofit organization that provides housing for people with chronic mental illness)

Investors

National Equity Fund
Edison Capital
Duquesne Power and Light

City of Philadelphia

*Wayne Spilove, Chairman, and Richard Tyler, Executive Director Philadelphia Historical Commission
*John Kromer, Director, Philadelphia Office of Housing and Community Development
*Noel Eisenstat, Executive Director, Redevelopment Authority
*Steve Mullen, Commerce Department
Richard Redding, Executive Director, City Planning Commission
*Fernando Gallard, Manager Retention, Mayor's Business Action Team
William Mifflin, Executive Director, Fairmount Park Commission

State of Pennsylvania

Aileen Demshock, Pennsylvania Housing Finance Agency
Janet Klein, Chairperson, Pennsylvania Museum and Historic Commission
*Vincent Hughes, State Legislator
*Chaka Fattah, US Congressperson, Pennsylvania 2nd district

Architects/Planners/Preservationists/Builders

*Robert P. Thomas, Partner, Campbell Thomas & Co. Architects
*George Thomas, Architectural Historian, University of Pennsylvania
*Edmund Bacon, former Executive Director, Philadelphia City Planning Commission
Ed Hillis, Dormas Construction
*Don Meginley, President, Preservation Alliance of Greater Philadelphia
Kathleen Milley, National Trust for Historic Preservation
Amy Frietag, Director, Fairmont Park Historic Preservation Trust

Tenants

*Mothers and children of Interim House
*Senior residents and families along Parkside Avenue

Other

*Mother Divine, Friends of Father Divine
*James Brown V, and Charlotte Brown, Parkside Preservation

PROJECT DESCRIPTION

HISTORY

The East Parkside neighborhood first attracted interest because of its proximity to America's first World's Fair, the 1876 Centennial Exposition, at nearby West Fairmont Park (Memorial Hall, directly opposite Parkside's mansions, is among the few remaining Exposition structures). Transit lines reached Parkside in the 1890s, making it an attractive location for early development. After the Exposition buildings were dismantled, the blocks along Parkside Avenue were developed by (and, for the most part, for) a group of German nouveau riche "beer barons" who had moved west from center-city neighborhoods. Frederick Poth built most of the mansions along Parkside Avenue in 1897, and in the following decades smaller, more modest homes rose on the side streets connecting Parkside Avenue and Girard Avenue.

In the 1920s the area underwent its first major demographic shift, receiving an influx of mostly Jewish, middle-class eastern European immigrants. The 1950s and 1960s brought another major population shift, to middle- and lower-income African Americans. There was significant disinvestment in the area as vandalism, arson, and abandonment diminished the community. These troubles in West Philadelphia, and in this neighborhood in particular, reflect the larger story of Philadelphia's growing urban problems over the past 30-40 years. The city saw its population drop by almost half in that period; East Parkside fared even worse, sliding from an estimated

10,000 in 1950 to 4,379 in 1997. The steepest decline in population occurred in the decade of the 1970s, when the area experienced a 41% drop.

James Brown IV and his wife Charlotte rented an apartment in Parkside in 1961, just as the change in ownership and ethnicity of the neighborhood had begun, and the abandonment and deterioration of the buildings was beginning to take hold. His landlord, William Henderson, had purchased two of the Parkside Avenue mansions. Brown learned the art of renovating historic properties by working with Henderson on that building, and honed these skills on the building he purchased in 1963 at 4218 Parkside for a hard-earned $12,000. The renovation of these buildings was closely tied to the heat and rhetoric of the 1960s civil rights movement and the desire of these young African Americans to do something that would make a material difference in the quality of their community. To increase his skill and understanding of the community development process, Brown quit his research job and took a position with the City's Redevelopment Authority to work under Director and well-known urban planner Ed Bacon.

Some of the larger mansions were abandoned and had begun to deteriorate visibly by 1967. Brown and Henderson "took it upon themselves to board up (the Landsdowne) and seal the doors," and they purchased the building later that year at auction. With the advent of the 1968 Housing Act, they formed the Parkside Development Corporation to rehabilitate the Landsdowne for low- and moderate-income people. The difficult rehabilitation was completed in 1972. By then, Brown had quit the Redevelopment Authority to become a full-time community developer. He and his partners purchased other buildings but found mortgage financing scarce until the mid-1980s, when banks came under local and federal pressure to make community development loans.

In 1982 a search for better ways to finance low-cost housing led to the idea of using historic tax credits to generate capital for development. In 1983 Brown and several partners formed the Parkside Historic Preservation Corporation (PHPC) and hired architectural historian George Thomas to research and complete the nomination form to place the district on the National Register of Historic Places. The district was approved in November of that

James Brown IV, Executive Director, Parkside Historic Preservation Corporation.

year. Soon after, with the help of University of Pennsylvania historic preservation students as interns, historically appropriate and energy-efficient improvements were made to the Landsdowne.

In 1986 Brown became engaged in a new effort that led to his biggest financial loss. City agency officials asked him to participate in a project to demonstrate the possibility of creating low-income units with a mix of city-financed low-interest loans, private financing, and historic tax credits. On assurances of support from the city, Brown borrowed several hundred thousand dollars from a private lender to begin the work on 10 of his buildings, only to see negotiations with the city fail over prevailing wages for construction workers. Faced with foreclosure, Brown obtained another loan for construction from Mellon Bank. When construction costs ran over budget, Mellon Bank refused to extend the loan. Eventually, in 1996, after extended negotiation and litigation, the properties were placed in receivership. In April 1999, Mellon offered those properties to Pennrose Properties, which is purchasing them for development.

In 1990 restoration of the remaining three major mansions on Parkside Avenue (one had been demolished, leaving the Brantwood, the Brentwood, and the Brantwood II) began with applications to the Local Initiatives Support Corporation (LISC) for pre-development funds, to the City for Community Block Grants support, and to the Federal Home Loan Bank for mortgages. The Brantwood was completed in 1993.

The Landsdowne Apartments restored in 1987.

Obtaining the Brentwood for restoration was more difficult since the use of federal funds mandated that the city use a proposal process to select developers. Brown was angered when PHPC lost the bid to a developer from outside the community, Pennrose Properties, a larger organization seen as more capable of undertaking the more extensive renovations of the Brentwood. PHPC, Brown felt, was clearly the legitimate developer in this community, and for a time they considered using community pressure to stand in the way of the development. (The clear consensus of officials is that PHPC could have stalled or stopped development if they wished.) Instead they agreed to partner with Pennrose, making use of Pennrose's financial resources and expertise and PHPC's community credentials and experience. Brentwood was completed in 1996, and Brantwood II became ready for occupancy in April, 1999. Ultimately, this was a good experience for PHPC. They have developed a solid relationship with Pennrose that is extending to other development projects throughout the neighborhood.

While Brown has been the most significant force in the redevelopment of Parkside, he has not been the only one. Five churches in the neighborhood have been closely involved in community welfare. Other players have also taken an interest and sometimes an active role in community development, including the Philadelphia Zoo, Habitat for Humanity, the Leidy School, Belmont Housing, and the 1260 Housing Corporation. In 1996 the Parkside Historic District Coalition was formed, with PHPC as a founding member, as a forum in which these groups could meet to inform each other about projects, plans, and concerns for the neighborhood. They have commissioned a neighborhood needs assessment report, and they are working together to increase and improve resident participation in planning.

Parkside garden gate detail

PROPERTIES DEVELOPED BY BROWN & ASSOCIATES IN PARKSIDE

Name	# Rental Units	Date of Work	Tenants	Owners/Developers
Landsdowne Apartments	48 units	Rehab, 1972 Restored, 1987 Restored 1991	Low-income, subsidized, and market-rate 50% tenants from 1260 Housing Corp, rest are Section 8 and market rate	Parkside Development Corp. Foreclosed by Mellon, 1996
Brantwood I	18 units 3 whole floor units	Restored 1993 Rehab 1994	PHMC female substance abusers and children PHMC Daycare, and staff offices	PHPC PHPC
Brentwood	43 units	restored 1996	Elderly (Section 8) and families (market rate)	Brentwood Parkside Assoc (Pennrose and PHPC as partners)
Brantwood II	16 units	April 1999	Market rate	Brantwood II Assoc (Pennrose and PHPC as partners)
Marlton Residences	25 units	June 1999	Adults with AIDS/HIV	Marlton Housing Partnership (Pennrose, PHPC and We the People Living with AIDS/HIV)

VISION

James Brown IV began by staking a claim in the neighborhood, buying and restoring buildings that seemed in danger of demolition. As his experience, confidence, and skill grew, he set his sights on saving the showplace street-front of Parkside Avenue. Later, as he evolved from an individual developer to a nonprofit community development corporation, he began to dream of restoring the entire neighborhood. Throughout these transitions, however, his effort has been marked by a long-term vision encompassing at least three main themes: social justice, conservation, and economic development. All three of these narratives demonstrate Brown's commitment to a neighborhood that he and his family have lived in for almost four decades.

One striking element of Brown's social vision was his determination to anchor the neighborhood with special needs housing. Mansions along Parkside have become homes for people with impaired

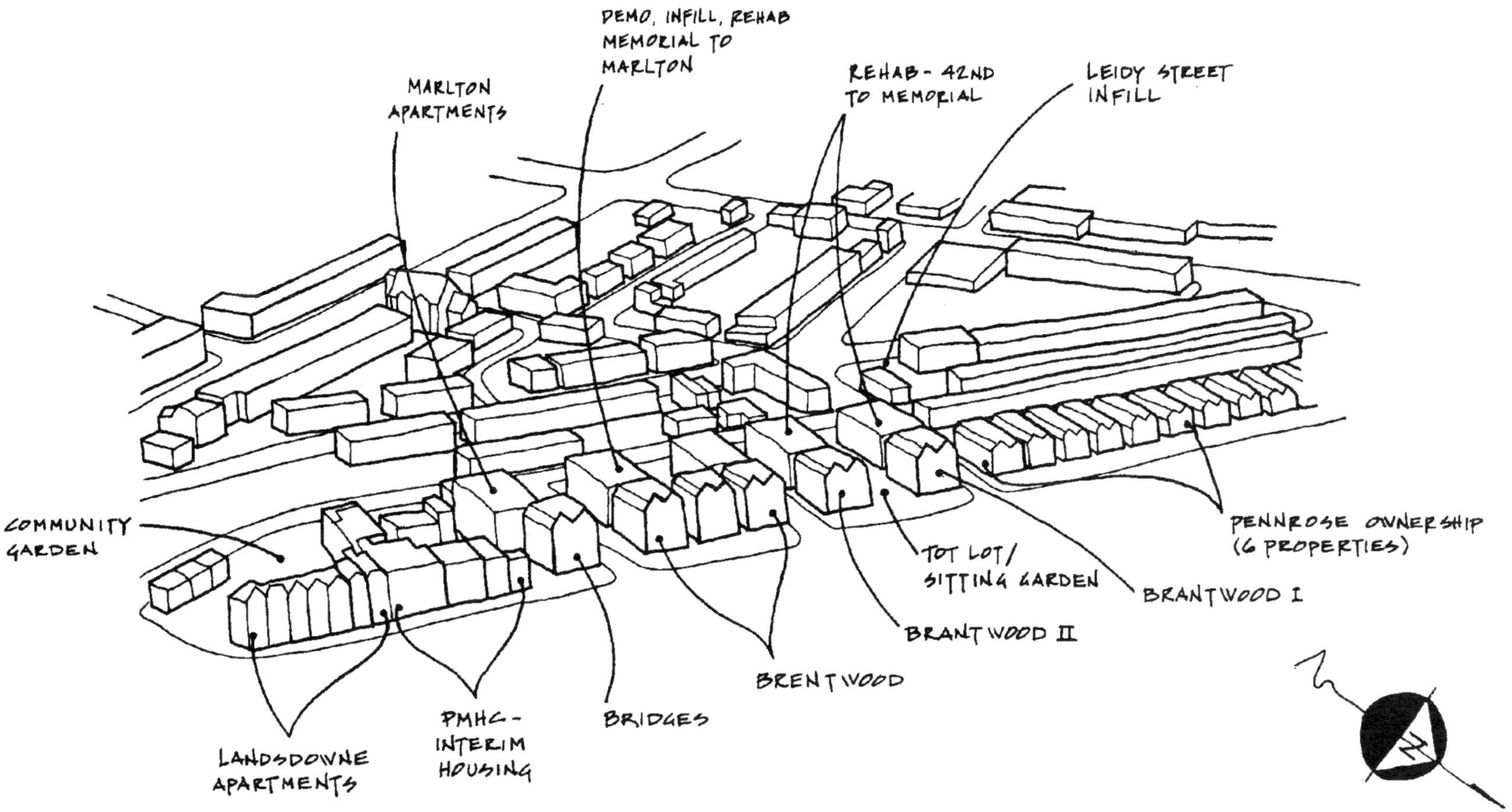

The location of properties developed by the Parkside Historic Preservation Corporation.

mobility (Belmont Housing Corporation), people with chronic mental illness (the 1260 Housing Corporation), women who were substance abusers and their children (Philadelphia Health Management Corporation, or PHMC) and, more recently, people with AIDS/HIV (We the People with AIDS/HIV). Since these mansions are some of the very finest buildings in Parkside (see "Renovations" below), their location helps reverse the tendency for the services they house to become associated with a "slum" area within an otherwise "respectable" neighborhood (thus the infamous "not-in-my-back-yard," or "NIMBY" syndrome). Instead, it is almost guaranteed that the mansions will remain the area's crowning jewels, offering services which are an important element of community life.

This special needs housing strategy points towards another related element of Brown's social vision: his commitment to inclusive planning. Although the Parkside community itself has had little direct involvement in the development process, the Selection Committee noted that Brown went out of his way to involve community service and advocacy groups in the project. While Brown clearly retained a great deal of authority in the relationship, the site visit team observed that support for Brown's actions among community leaders was wide and deep. Since the still-devastated neighborhood is not yet home to a politically active population, Brown's efforts to engage local social services as an intermediate strategy seemed appropriate. It would be fully in keeping with PHPC's social vision to help foster a politically viable neighborhood

Detailing on the Marlton restoration.

Typical neighborhood street with construction in progress

community through such efforts, and then incorporate it into the ongoing process.

Brown's social vision is closely related to his conception of *conservation*, which is a much more comprehensive term in his usage than it is ordinarily understood to be. In part, it has meant using the existing building stock instead of razing and building anew. But it has also meant something more fundamental than that. As one interviewee explained, "The neighborhood was a drug and crime zone sprinkled with homeless people. To you or me it might have looked as if no one lived there. Brown looked at the same place, and saw the same people, but he recognized them as local residents, and built a home for them as well as for newer residents."

For Brown conservation meant using existing building stock to anchor renewal, but it has also meant ensuring that those properties remained available to neighborhood residents and programs. One consequence has been that, although there were relatively few people living in the neighborhood from the outset, virtually none of them have been displaced. This vision of rebuilding a neighborhood for the people who are already there sits at the core of Brown's approach and is a good part of what makes this urban intervention so powerful.

As in all successful community development projects, there is an economic component to Brown's central vision. Brown sees his project as a way to "capitalize" an African American community in

Renovations along Marlton Avenue are in progress

a way that is reminiscent of the social criticism and political goals of the later civil rights movement. His goal is to create a viable African American neighborhood, one in which residents can achieve some degree of autonomy through the creation of wealth. (As a major investor in the area, he considers himself one such wealth-seeking resident.) Skilled in attaining government funding, he remains wary of the strings and formal planning that must accompany such money and prefers to focus on the neighborhood's natural assets to lure private investment. Brown and some others see Parkside as ripe for development, offering not just a compendium of problems but tangible assets – particularly location (see "Context" below). Although he has begun with low- and moderate-income, and special needs housing, Brown eventually hopes to create market-rate units to accompany a more general economic rebirth of the neighborhood. This economic focus again reflects his commitment to the area, and adds a necessary pragmatic element to his overall vision of conservation.

Finally, historic preservation plays a key role in Brown's vision, although the site visit team felt that it was clearly a secondary concern compared to other goals. The Selection Committee concurred, impressed with how the project was "about how people come together rather than being about objects." Even so, as with every part of the project, this economic strategy (devised to get historic preservation tax credits) has been incorporated into the broader vision. The attention to detail required by this type of renovation has resulted in truly beautiful buildings, buildings that

The Brentwood from Fairmount Park

not only serve to avert a "NIMBY" response, but also stand as eloquent symbols for the care, love, and commitment felt for this neighborhood. The decision to house low income or special needs residents in these renovated buildings reinforces the basic elements of Brown's vision in a way that perhaps no other strategy could have.

Organization/Leadership

> *Transformation of the almost 4,000 structures in the area will take 25 years, Brown estimates, and he's in for the duration. 'That's my goal and my career. Unless I go bankrupt, I'll stay right here and see it through.'*
>
> Historic Preservation Magazine

James Brown IV is the animating force and visionary leader of redevelopment in Parkside. The nonprofit community development corporation, PHPC, is the most important vehicle for implementing his vision. Brown functions as the head of PHPC, works within the area as a private developer as he has for over 30 years, serves as a member of the Parkside Historic Community Coalition, is a member of the Fairmont Park Property Committee, and acts as a consultant or unofficial advisor to other organizations operating in the area. PHPC largely works with for-profit (Pennrose Properties) and nonprofit (PHMC, 1260 Housing) partners to rehabilitate and restore properties. It has a board of directors made up of local residents and members of local organizations. Their role is largely to review and consider issues, support, lobby, and ratify decisions.

It would not be an exaggeration to call Brown's leadership style heroic – a Selection Committee member remarked that if the Rudy Bruner Award were an "Urban Pioneer" award, Brown would certainly win it hands down. He has led by example and by perseverance, over time and through adversity. His commitment to the area – he has lived and worked there for nearly four decades – has given him a prominent, even inspirational, presence within the community, and has lent credibility to his efforts. He has carefully cultivated a deep set of political roots, working closely with nearly every local grassroots community organization and maintaining ties to the government as well (an Assemblyman opened his interview with the site visit team by stating, with only a little irony, "Whatever Mr. Brown wants"). Clearly, he is trusted and admired, and his standing in the community has made it easy for the residents to accept his judgment on NIMBY issues. A site visit team member suggested that it might be convenient to think of Brown as the unofficial Mayor of Parkside.

As important as Brown and the PHPC are, other organizations play important roles in the area. Most are represented in the Parkside Historic District Coalition (PHDC), a loosely bound coalition of institutions within East Parkside. The coalition functions mainly to maintain open communication and cooperation among its members, and is seeking to create channels of contact with residents. PHDC has explicitly avoided joint projects or more formal relationships in favor of maintaining a forum in which members can keep each other informed of their plans. Brown explains that once you have formal plans and structures, you have to divide up the pie, and this generally leads to conflict. It also can foreclose opportunities that you didn't know that you had. Thus both Brown's own board and PHDC keep a somewhat improvisational organizational style, maintaining an ability to respond to opportunities as they arise. "It is in the doing that the idea comes," explained former Executive Director of the City Planning Commission Ed Bacon.

The model here is of strong but not overly structured leadership, decentralized in the sense that community-wide development decisions are made by a number of different organizations, with Brown and PHPC being the largest and most active. Brown has the respect, and the ear, of important officials at all levels of city government and beyond, as well as of neighborhood leaders. He has kept his focus on his own significant but limited set of projects, and has not attempted to control or oversee everything in the community. The progress that has been achieved, and that is poised to accelerate in the near future, has been the result of a number of neighborhood groups operating in concert but independently: the churches, Habitat for Humanity, and other nonprofits and developers. In this respect the lack of powerful centralized control has been a strength, allowing a number of players to pursue solutions simultaneously.

Another way Brown's leadership has been strengthened through dilution has been the addition of Pennrose Properties into the mix. When PHPC moved from relatively small-scale projects like the Landsdowne and the Brantwood to the much larger Brentwood, the government rebuffed them in favor of the larger and more experienced Pennrose. After some initial anger (see "History"), Brown made the best of this situation, partnering with Pennrose for the Brentwood and future projects. As John Rosenfield and Robert Totaro of Pennrose explained it, the partnership is a marriage of "street savvy" and "suit savvy": Brown is good at local and city politics, and has the support of the community, while Pennrose has experience at getting state low-income tax credits (they had already done more than 50 low-income projects with a high rate of success). PHPC gained Pennrose's capital, national reputation, experience, and ability to put a deal together; Pennrose gained PHPC's help in getting local support for zoning, community development block grants, and HUD "HOME" grants.

DESIGN

Urban Context

East Parkside is a compact, relatively isolated neighborhood in the northeastern corner of West Philadelphia, whose population is 90% African American. Filling about 20 blocks, in includes approximately 1,500 homes and a score or so of other buildings including churches, stores, a fire station, a school, and a funeral home. It is bordered to the west by the city Zoo, to the east by an empowerment zone, to the north by the enormous Fairmont Park, and to the south by a deteriorated neighborhood giving way to heavy development around the University of Pennsylvania.

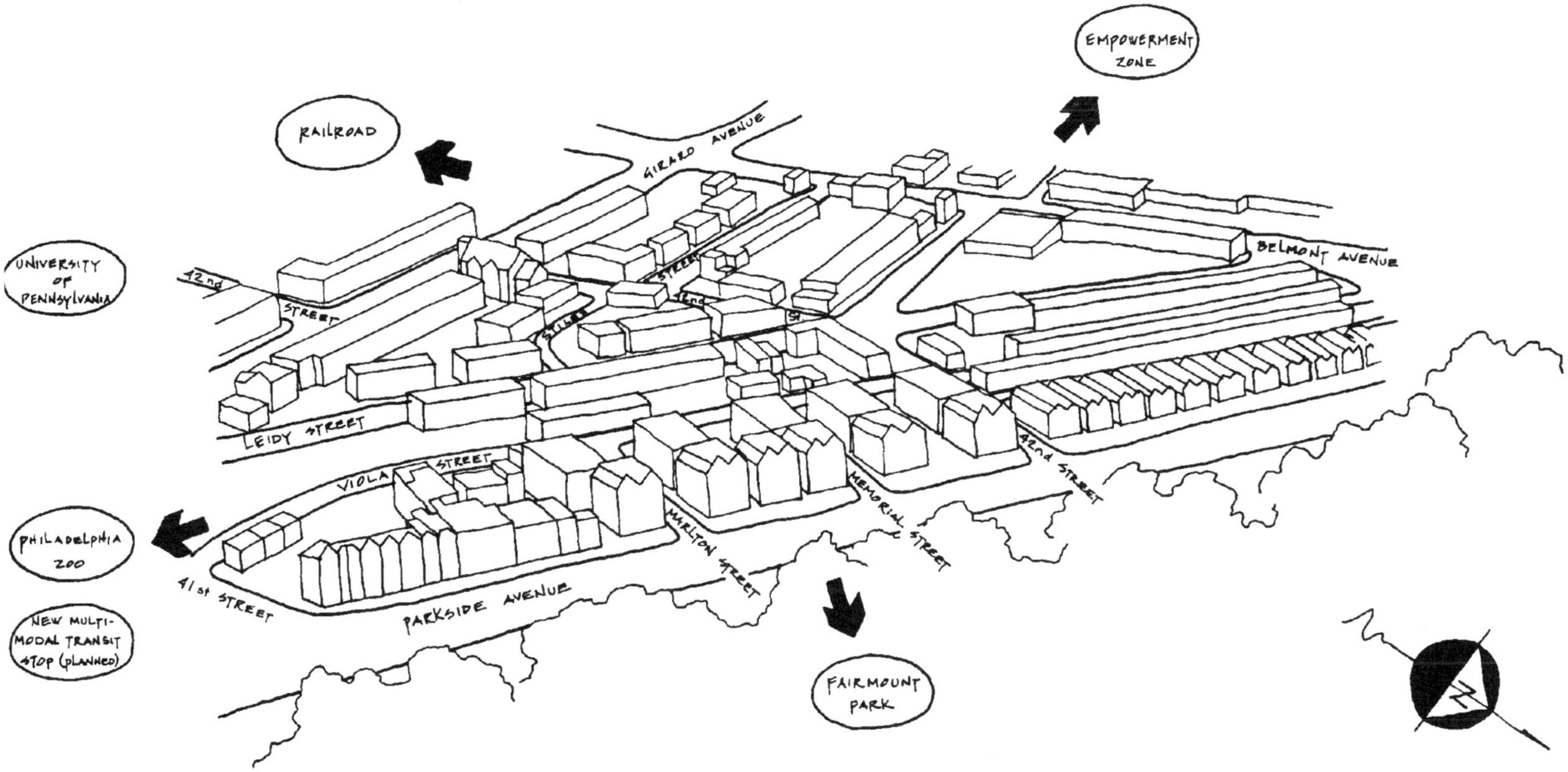

The Parkside neighborhood is strategically located adjacent to Fairmount Park, the Zoo, the proposed new multi-modal transit station, the Philadelphia Empowerment Zone, and the University of Pennsylvania.

The neighborhood's location offers several advantages. A new multi-modal transit stop planned for the nearby Zoo, encompassing Amtrak, trolley, light rail, and bus, promises convenient commuting in a city where 30% of the families do not own cars. The new transit lines will make even easier the already convenient access to downtown, and will add commuting possibilities for Reading, the mall, and the empowerment zone as well. The neighborhood is also close to Fairmont Park and important park facilities such as the Mann Music Center. In the past, however, the very enormity of the Park (it is larger than Manhattan Island) has made maintenance difficult, presenting a key obstacle to renewal. Brown has also addressed this problem to some extent, participating in and collaborating with the Philadelphia Green, the Pennsylvania Horticultural Society, the Fairmont Park Historic Trust, Friends of Philadelphia's Parks, and other related organizations.

Despite these assets, however, it is important to recognize just how far Parkside has to go to become a healthy neighborhood. The vacancy rate in this area is 22.7%, more than double the Philadelphia average, and real estate values are the lowest in West Philadelphia. Home ownership is rare. As of the 1990 census the median income was about $16,000 (65% of city median income). A significant minority (34%) of current residents live below the poverty level. There is little evidence of a coherent, unified neighborhood; most residents who have stayed endure low income and social dysfunction. They are largely people without the resources to leave. Sixty-seven percent of all families are headed by a single parent, and unemployment is 16.7% (nearly double the city rate). The few retail businesses remaining in the area, mostly on Girard (the "main street"), offer little in quality services or job possibilities to residents.

Brown's renovations, while still too small in scope to effect an immediate transformation of the neighborhood, have nevertheless had a noticeable impact, particularly along Parkside Avenue itself. Because it is a heavily traveled corridor to the city from western suburbs, the Avenue had become a symbol of urban decay; it now stands as a symbol of urban renewal and rejuvenation.

An Historical Neighborhood

> *"No one in their right mind would ever try to rebuild this building!"*
> Ed Bacon, former Executive Director,
> Philadelphia City Planning Commission.

The original housing stock, especially along Parkside Avenue, was distinguished and unique in Philadelphia. The German beer barons who established Parkside Avenue made use of German and Flemish revival styles, rather than those of the English Victorian era that dominate the rest of the city. In part this reflected their choice of an upstart architect, Frederick Poth, who worked outside the fashionable "South of Market" area for nouveau riche like the beer barons.

The several blocks of Parkside Avenue housed the brewmeisters themselves in the largest and finest of the neighborhood's homes.

The Brantwood II on Parkside Avenue

Their ornate mansions, largely intact today, present a unified and coherent face to the avenue and the park. The preference for strong ornamentation concentrated on the street front, for porch fronts to emphasize the suburban quality, and for style elements derived from florid Dutch and German architecture, contrasts with the plain red brick buildings of Rittenhouse Square. On the eastern edge of Parkside Avenue, developers built 14 four-story copper and terra cotta trimmed Pompeiian brick double buildings that look like mansions but were instead apartments. The block is unified by the row of elaborately molded terra cotta porch fronts. Farther west on Parkside is a group of three-story porch front doubles, again presenting a unified appearance to the street.

As one moves away from the park, the next layer of housing was intended for middle managers in the booming brewery business. Beyond that are row houses and smaller units for workers, which sit next to what used to be the industrial area itself. The houses on these secondary streets are more modest in scale and materials, but are similar in style and ornate decoration, with gable fronts and porches.

The Renovations

While the original housing stock may have been lavish and beautiful, perhaps the most important fact about Parkside's buildings from a modern-day perspective was their extremely deteriorated condition before Brown's intervention. The Brentwood, for example, was entirely burnt out, little more than a shell. Conditions in the neighborhood were so poor, however, that Brown actually saw the Brentwood's state as a relative advantage: the fires had gotten rid of most of the lead paint, reducing abatement costs. Such an attitude, while pragmatic, points to the sorry state of the area's unburned buildings – to make a gutted one so appealing. In short, these were serious, fundamental renovations to salvage buildings that, as Ed Bacon remarked, "No one in their right mind" would consider saving. "If I had studied planning," Brown laughed, "I never would have gotten involved." From Brown's perspective, if he had had the training of a conventional planner, he would have demolished to build new structures or looked elsewhere to do this work.

In this light, the care that has been taken to maintain and restore the exterior style and detail of the original is impressive. Gargoyles have been recast, decorative moldings duplicated, cornices replaced. New and in-fill buildings lack the detail of the historic structures but attempt to copy the scale and line of the originals. The interior designs follow the exterior detail where necessary; interior walls, for example, do not intersect bay windows.

Even so, the Selection Committee felt that the quality of the restorations had diminished in the more recent projects. The Landsdowne, a huge, four-story mansion with minarets and bays in

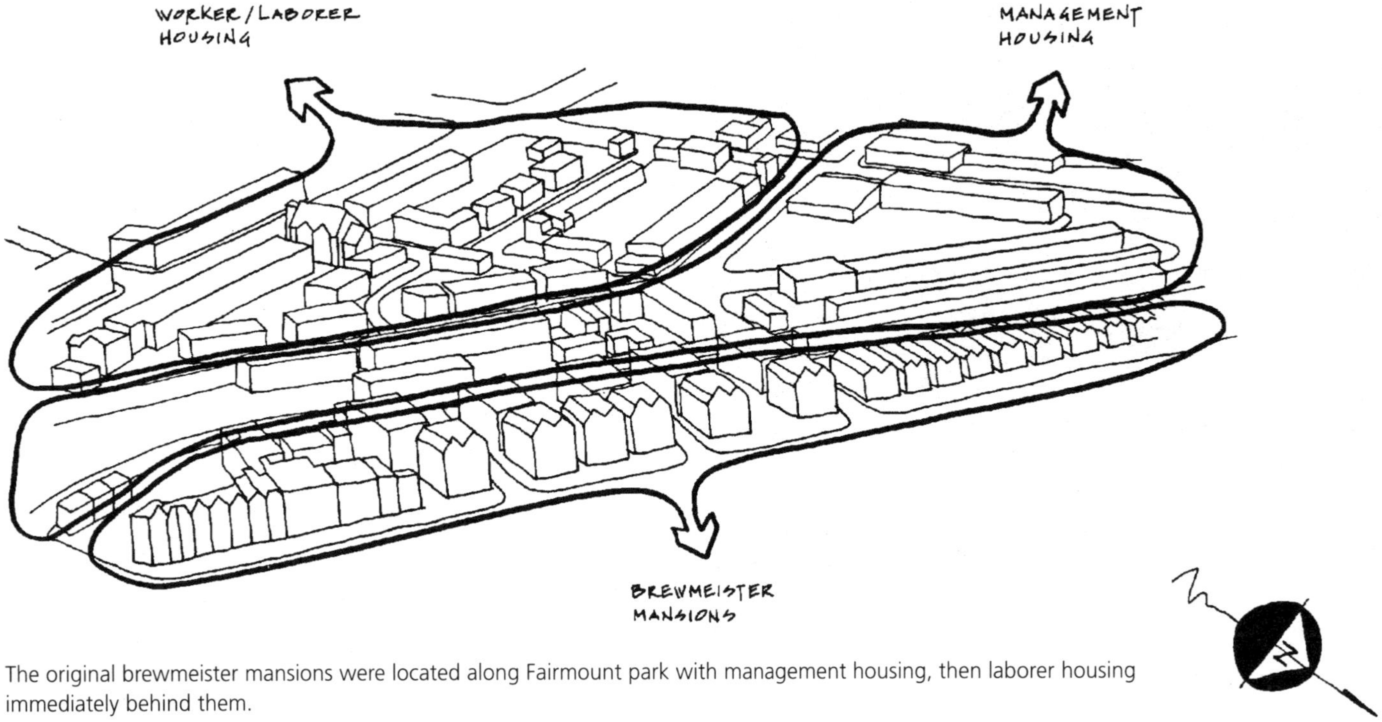

The original brewmeister mansions were located along Fairmount park with management housing, then laborer housing immediately behind them.

a "grandly eclectic" style decorated with pressed tin cornices, traceries windows, and a variety of textures "recalling the picturesque Queen Anne," has been restored in magnificent style and minute detail. The Brantwood and later buildings, however, show evidence of less attention to detail. One finds, for example, beautiful oval windows, but with ordinary flat molding in the place of the original ornamental woodwork.

In addition, the interiors of the buildings tend to be fairly conventional modern apartments out of keeping with the historic facades. They are certainly functional, and are well-designed with the special needs of their residents in mind. The Brentwood, for instance, has a ground floor lounge where the elderly and family residents can meet and socialize. Large family-sized apartments are on the ground level, with separate entrances, so children can enter directly without running through apartment hallways. Other units have been made fully wheelchair accessible. Nonetheless, the Selection Committee noted that the impressiveness of restoring such devastated buildings was diminished somewhat by these ordinary interiors.

The restorations also create occasional jarring juxtapositions of images. One can stand inside a new living room of a grand, restored mansion and look out the back window to see, several yards away, a rotting and collapsing structure. Brown has managed to take advantage of some of these discontinuities. For example, a

Original details on Brentwood

View of the restored Brentwood from Brantwood II, illustrating the simplified molding details on the oval windows.

vacant lot, the site of a demolished mansion, separates the Brentwood 1 and 2. It is being turned into a small park that will serve as an entranceway and provide a pleasant view for many units. Archways reflecting the rounded arches of the surrounding buildings are being designed for the street frontage facing Fairmont Park.

FINANCING

Approximately $21 million worth of development has been invested in this area to date. The expensive materials and high degree of care required by restoration efforts have made the cost of renovations about 20-25% higher on the Parkside mansions than typical Philadelphia rental units. A 1996 publication by the City of Philadelphia Office of Housing and Community Development notes that rehabilitation of long-vacant properties in Philadelphia ranges from $70,000 to $150,000, and cites the Brentwood as an example of a project worth the extra cost because "it serves as a gateway and protective barrier for a low-rise residential neighborhood behind the Avenue," and because its demolition would lead to increased security problems, vacancies, and abandonment. Noel Eisenstat, Executive Director of the Redevelopment Authority, explained it this way: "Brown's work costs way too much – it goes against the market – but it's okay because he's taking a stand on a strategic piece of property, a gateway site for the whole city."

Financing of these projects has been driven by several realities. No one within this community has had the financial resources to support rehabilitations and restorations (one of Brown's stated goals is to help build some of this capacity in the neighborhood). Brown needed to begin by restoring the most expensive showpiece buildings to create confidence in the neighborhood before development could move on to more modest buildings. The market (in terms of the cost of loans and the income that rentals can bring) is not yet able to support this development. As a result, PHPC has had to use several strategies to create the necessary funding. Brown was an early user of both low-income and historic preservation tax credits as a way to generate capital for development. Two-thirds of the cost of his developments are typically covered by private sources. In addition, to make the investment more attractive for limited partners and to increase PHPC's long-term equity stake, they encourage investors to donate their remaining share to the corporation when the asset no longer carries any paper value, giving limited partnership investors one last tax deduction.

Brown believes that subsidized development creates dependence and leaves developers and residents subject to official whims and policy changes; for that reason he is especially eager to finance with other sources (such as equity partnerships). PHPC has received seven major private foundation grants ranging from $5,000 to $125,000, the most significant ones from the Pew Charitable Trust and the Connelly Foundation. PHPC has partnered with for-profit and nonprofit organizations with financial resources and/or access to other funding sources (such as Pennrose and the Pennsylvania Historical and Museum Corporation). They also have been successful at getting public loans and some private grants to support projects. As the development of the neighborhood advances and reaches greater maturity, they hope to use the equity in early sites to support market rate loans for future construction.

Brown's formula makes financing these projects straightforward. He uses low-income and historic preservation tax credits, equity from general and limited partners, and combines them with loans and grants. It is interesting to note that the project has benefited both from Pennrose's experience in the tough competition for low-income credits, and from Philadelphia's strong history in this area (with about 10% of the state's population, the city typically receives nearly half of the state low-income tax credits). The city has supported development by extending the maximum on community development block grant subsidies by 30%, giving Parkside $2 million in Community Development Bank (CDB) grants. The city Redevelopment Authority also supports projects in East Parkside by turning over land and structures seized for tax default. City officials see this approach as a model of community development via public support for nonprofit/for-profit partnerships.

USES/SOURCES FOR THE BRANTWOOD

Uses	
Construct Cost	$1,890,600
Fees	$192,000
Misc.	$26,000
Construction Financing & Charges	$37,000
Project Reserves	$37,000
Developer's Fee & OH	$411,484
Syndicating Fees & Expenses	$43,140
Other	$5,100
Total	**$2,642,324**

Sources	
Mortgage	$825,000
CDBG	$372,700
Historic Tax Credits	$1,445,624
Equity	**$2,643,324**

One member of the Selection Committee noted that, while this fundraising is impressive, it is not particularly difficult to raise this kind of developer money for rental units; the true challenge comes in making the leap from a renting to an owning population.

Parkside Preservation and the City of Philadelphia

The Parkside effort has clearly been led from within the neighborhood; indeed, as both the site visit team and the Selection Committee recognized, Brown is wary of public funding and has gone out of his way to ask for as little as possible from the city (he did not want to be part of the Empowerment Zone next door, for example). The City of Philadelphia has, however, played the important role of development facilitator at crucial times. The city has been helpful, especially in recent years, in channeling federal housing support in the form of low-income tax credits and CDB Grants. The City also supported and ratified the historic district status for the neighborhood, which was critical for making use of historic preservation tax credits. It played a critical role in bringing Pennrose Properties into the neighborhood by requiring a bidding process for developing the Brantwood, and then helped to bring Pennrose and PHPC together as partners to complete the project.

City efforts have not always been so helpful. Brown's difficulties with the Mellon bank began in 1986 when city officials initially encouraged him to buy homes for a demonstration project of public-private funding and then later terminated its involvement.

FUTURE PLANS

Development momentum is now moving off of Parkside Avenue and down the side streets of the district, and Brown anticipates that the rest of the rehabilitation of the neighborhood will take the better part of a decade. Progress is accelerating, however, and that timeline may shorten due to several factors: the resources, expertise, and drive added by PHPC's private partner, Pennrose Properties; PHPC's recognition and growing reputation, which makes it easier to garner support from the city and other organizations; and the slowly strenghtening coalition of groups adding their energies to Brown's casue. Members of the Parkside Historical District Coalition and another, non-related private developer have significant programs of development underway. Virtually every block in the triangle has properties that are active, that have been acquired for impending development, or that are under consideration. Successful implementation of the Zoo's transportation center proposal could significantly accelerate progress.

When the new building for Interim House, developed jointly by PHPC and PHMC, is finished, work on Parkside Avenue will be essentially complete and, as envisioned early on, the effort will move to the interior blocks. The partnership of PHPC with Pennrose Properties plans to complete 60 units of senior housing on Girard Avenue east of 40th Street through rehabilitation and new, in-fill buildings; 12 properties for rehabilitation on Viola between 42nd Street and Memorial; rehabilitation of older structures and addition of new in-fill buildings on the South Side of Girard, west of 42nd Street; and development of a commercial retail area on 41st Street between Girard & Poplar.

In addition, they plan to take advantage of a proposed new law that would allow the use of low-income tax credits for home ownership by creating new market-rate housing on Leidy Street, after this street has been declared an urban renewal area. This would be PHPC's first foray into home ownership development. Brown expects land to be given to PHPC by the city and hopes to use state and Redevelopment Authority tax-exempt bonds for financing.

The new Interim House facility should provide several important side benefits for the community. There is a plan for public community space in this facility. Brown hopes to have a satellite program from a community college available there, as well as a day care center. Also, since special needs housing provides health care jobs for people in the community, there is also discussion of providing a health care job training center at this site.

Habitat for Humanity, working with the Belmont Housing Corporation and the First African Presbyterian Church, will continue to create occupant-owned, sweat-equity homes and plans to develop the entire block of Styles between 42nd Street and Belmont. It will also develop four lots behind the First African church into a community park. Private developer Leonard Goldman and his partner Harold Thomas have also begun buying and developing property in and near the area. They now control 30 properties, mostly on Girard and 42nd Street, at the south end of the district, to be developed for low-income rental housing. Habitat for Humanity and Belmont Housing are putting together the financing to acquire Belmont Village, a 12-unit apartment house, and to create six accessible units for Inglis House clients, offices for Habitat, and a dormitory for volunteer workers.

The 1260 Housing Corporation has constructed ten new row houses on Thompson Street that will serve as transitional housing for individuals with chronic mental illness. Christ Community Baptist Church has yet to define plans to develop property it owns on Girard between 40th and 41st Streets.

Possibly the most exciting new developments center around the Philadelphia Zoo. The Zoo and others (including Brown) are lobbying hard to reopen a long abandoned railroad stop near its front entrance. This, along with a planned new light rail line, would create a multi-modal transportation center (Amtrak, trolley, light rail, bus) that would carry customers to and from the Zoo, create easy access to work opportunities for area residents, and could become the focal point for a retail center. Conversely, improved public transportation will improve accessibility to the neighborhood from other parts of Philadelphia.

ASSESSING PROJECT SUCCESS

HOW WELL PROJECT MEETS ITS OWN GOALS

□ *To arrest a neighborhood's deterioration.*

Parkside Preservation has been relatively successful in this regard. Physical and architectural improvements are significant on Parkside Avenue and are beginning to be felt on the interior blocks, where significant change is likely to occur in the next few years. There is a great deal left to do, but it appears that the neighborhood has "hit bottom" and is beginning to recover. The out-migration of residents has slowed or ceased, and there is some anecdotal evidence that people are beginning to move into the area. It is also important to note that, while crime is an important issue in this neighborhood, there has been very little vandalism in project buildings, suggesting tacit community support. The residents we talked to did not feel overwhelmingly fearful or concerned – women might be wary of walking at night, but not particularly during the day, alone or with their children. Brown suggested that one reason that police respond better in this neighborhood than in some others is because they know that Parkside is willing to follow through with prosecution. (See also "Impact" below).

- *To provide a standard of housing not normally available to the poor.*

The quality of the renovated housing is good and is a major improvement over existing neighborhood conditions. Much of the housing in the best buildings is for special needs groups. Future development will be aimed less at special needs residents and more toward adding additional low-income and market-rate housing.

Marlton Apartments under renovation for We Are the People With AIDS/HIV.

- *To bring historic preservation into an area not ordinarily desirable to developers.*

PHPC has succeeded in saving and restoring buildings that almost certainly would otherwise have been demolished. When Brown started there was no development money for this neighborhood and especially not for the significant mansions that are quite expensive to restore and renovate. Changes in the tax code helped, but even so, it was Brown's perseverance that made the difference.

- *To support the socio-economic and ethnic composition of the area.*

As yet little pressure has emerged from other socio-economic or ethnic groups to move into or gentrify the neighborhood. This is probably more due to physical and economic conditions in the neighborhood than to specific strategies to avoid gentrification. It is significant, however, that premier space in restored mansions on Parkside has been leased to services that support the neighborhood population.

OTHER MEASURES OF SUCCESS

Sustainability

Concerns about the sustainability of this project and its unique network of organizations and leaders exist for several reasons: because so much is focused on the leadership of James Brown; because development cannot be supported exclusively by private funding (and market-rate rentals and purchases are still partly dependent on subsidies and tax credits); because of the lack of a formal, comprehensive plan; and because East Parkside still seems a long way from becoming a solid, cohesive community.

To be sure, Brown remains central to these efforts in many respects, and his loss would be a serious blow to progress. There are, however, reasons to think that development here will continue and flourish. James Brown V is apparently being groomed to take over his father's position. Also, solid and long-term community leaders in the Parkside Historic Coalition could fill some, if not all, of any leadership void. Significant momentum for development also exists here – not enough to ensure continuation, but enough to ease the path for a next generation of leaders. Funding sources such as equity from Pennrose and tax incentives do not appear to be lessening, and may expand to cover private ownership efforts. Lastly, while the project lacks a formal neighborhood-wide comprehensive planning document, Coalition members share a common understanding of goals, values, and future directions. Nonetheless, the Selection Committee emphasized what seems obvious but remains crucial: the project's continual progress depends on the participation of people willing to work as hard as Brown. Such a scenario, though far from impossible, is certainly not given.

The other measure of sustainability stressed by the Selection Committee will be found in the success of efforts in the neighborhood to go beyond rental housing to homeownership. From the Selection Committee perspective, the creation of low-income and preservation credit rental units is an easier task than attracting ownership investment. At the present, none of the efforts of Parkside preservation have addressed the issue of ownership, nor is there a long term strategy in place to achieve it.

Impact

It would be inappropriate to suggest that a few buildings in this small neighborhood outside downtown can or should have a city-wide impact, with respect to finances or overall livability. Certainly this project has the attention and support of city government, from agency heads to elected officials. For the city, these are visible and symbolically important blocks. Where they once conveyed an image of urban decay and deterioration, now they are put forward to showcase change and renewal. Parkside is also held up as a model of how local African-American communities can create and nurture their own capacity to foster development.

In addition, Brown's expertise has been used to support development in other areas. He has consulted and advised other neighborhoods and other development projects, and Fairmont Park officials say they have used their relations with Parkside as a model for dealing with "friends of the park" groups in other parts of town. At a recent, informal meeting in the mayor's office, city officials were surprised that community representatives from another part of town (North Philadelphia), who they expected to feel competitive with PHPC, instead praised Brown's work and demanded that the city provide him more funds and greater support. Brown seems to be viewed throughout the city as an inspiration and a community resource.

Two business owners on the western edge of this area say that PHPC has made it easier for business people to consider moving to this part of Philadelphia. Leonard Goldman, a private developer who has begun buying and rehabilitating modest homes in and near the southern edge of this district, indicated that PHPC's success has reduced the risk he and his partners face in coming into this area. It has increased interest in prospects here and made it easier for them to syndicate their investments. He typically drives potential investors along Parkside Avenue to impress them with change in the area. Goldman also indicated that in the past year he has seen some private owners in the area beginning to fix up their own homes. Principals from Habitat for Humanity also credit Brown with helping them navigate the city's bureaucratic maze to get started in the neighborhood.

Perhaps the most important impact of Parkside Preservation has been on the neighborhood itself and its near-moribund community. This is appropriate, given Brown's core commitment to conserving the area. There is evidence that neighborhood institutions are returning: the First Avenue Presbyterian and the Annex Christ churches, for example, have been restored. The community school has been renovated. A number of interviewees mentioned lower crime rates and a friendly atmosphere. There are, then, hopeful signs that Brown has succeeded in getting the area to take its first steps towards the ultimate dream of a thriving, diverse working - class neighborhood. Nonetheless, the Selection Committee felt quite strongly that one of the hardest obstacles yet remains: making the transition from a rental to an owning population. At this stage, the Committee conceded, Parkside does not seem "ready for home ownership," but without this key ingredient there is a significant limit to future revitalization. Thus, as one Committee member noted, there is "much pioneering left to go" before Parkside could be considered fully recovered.

Leadership and Vision

A theme that permeates this project is the ability of one person to make an impact. What has made Brown's leadership so valuable has not simply been his role as charismatic leader; rather, it has been his commitment to that role over decades of diligence. He and his family have lived in the neighborhood throughout its very worst

Typical Parkside neighborhood view

years. He has pursued creative economic strategies, but never any that conflict with his loyalty to conserving the existing place and protecting the people who live in it. And he has continually been willing to incorporate other players as they came onto the scene, even if they initially presented apparently hostile or competitive faces, as Pennrose did. It is these qualities that have built Brown's standing in the community, providing a model of "urban pioneering" that supports the community as well as changing it.

This kind of leadership reveals the related value of commitment to place. It is significant that Parkside reflects nearly 40 years of efforts centered on a single neighborhood. Such an investment of time and energy, and the continuous cooperation with local organizations, were more than the makings of a leader; they were also the concrete expressions of a commitment to a place. This kind of genuine caring for Parkside has been a crucial element of Brown's success, and would seem to be an important value for any project aiming to renew the spirit as well as the buildings of a damaged area.

Values Reflected in Development Process

Brown's commitment, as indicated earlier, has not been just to the place. Still echoing the fire and rhetoric of his 1960s civil rights era-roots, he has indicated that one of his goals is to strive for equality – symbolically, contractually, and financially – for African Americans in these projects. It is critical, he feels, for the community to build independence from government subsidies and outside funding to foster self-determination for the community. "How do we get away from subsidization? Little by little it is important to prove that we can create development in the inner city and that we can support ourselves in the open market. Otherwise we subject ourselves to the whims of politicians and agencies."

Another important theme has been the effort to be inclusive in process and design. As noted earlier, Brown has invited community participation to the extent possible in Parkside, and has been rewarded with broad and deep support from community organizations. He has shown a serious interest in developing this participation even further once the neighborhood attains a state that can support a politically aware population. Even without the direct involvement of community residents, work with service providers has supported a rich diversity of residents (although still few from the middle class). Rather than shying away from groups such as AIDS/HIV patients, the mentally ill, the physically disabled, and substance abusers, Parkside has embraced them, and even used their presence to anchor buildings and stabilize the community. To be sure, accommodating these groups had a utilitarian side – these were populations that often had access to sources of funding because of their special needs. Their presence made it easier to fund expensive projects, especially early in the process, and they provided many tenants in an overbuilt market. But it also true that Brown has sought diversity and has looked for ways to integrate these groups into the community.

Lastly, Parkside Preservation has owed its success in no small part to the organic nature of the design process. Brown has shied away from government funding as much because of its demand for concrete plans as for its fostering of economic dependence. He has skillfully maintained good relations among all the players by refusing to define the "pie" over whose pieces fights might erupt. Instead, he has preached the value of taking opportunities as they arise. Thus, for example, historic preservation was a way to get funding, but became an eloquent statement of commitment to the area's special needs population. A site visit team member reported that, like all good placemakers, Brown has balanced social justice and economic strategies, using the former to guide and the latter to power his projects.

FOR FURTHER INFORMATION

Thomas W. Sweeney, "Steady progress revitalizes Parkside: Distressed Philadelphia finds a champion," *Historic Preservation News* (vol. 33(5), June 1993, p. 20-21).

Susan Morse, "Mansions reborn: A Trust-aided rehab produces much-needed low-income housing in Philadelphia," *Historic Preservation,* (vol. 41(5), Sept.-Oct. 1989, p. 59-62).

Mark Jenkins, "His lifetime goal: Saving neighborhood (Parkside, Philadelphia)," *Historic Preservation.* (vol. 37, June 1985, p. 30).

Zane Miller and Bruce Tucker, *Changing Plans for America's Inner Cities: Cincinnati's Over-the-Rhine and Twentieth-Century Urbanism* (Columbus: Ohio State University Press, 1998). An historical narrative of city planning in Cincinnati, highlighting among other things the use of historic preservation as an economic and community development tool.

Related Rudy Bruner Award Winners

(For full bibliographic cites, please see Introduction)

Quality Hill in Kansas City, Missouri (1987 cycle). The renovation and redevelopment of this historic district adjacent to downtown was directed by a private developer who structured a partnership with the city and 20 local companies.

Ocean Drive Improvement Project, Miami Beach, Florida (1991 cycle). The preservation and revitalization of a 15-block, 26-acre ocean front historic district of Art Deco hotels and apartments overseen by the City Beach Office of Historic Preservation and Urban Design.

Betts-Longworth Historic District, Cincinnati, Ohio (1993 cycle). A preservation-based redevelopment plan for a downtown "mini-neighborhood" containing some of the city's oldest homes and encouraging participation of minority developers and contractors.

Lowerton, Saint Paul, Minnesota (1995 cycle). The redevelopment of a historic district near the downtown by a small private nonprofit organization that has created a lively, mixed income and mixed use area, including retail, office, and low-mod and market rate housing.

Cleveland Historic Warehouse District (1997 cycle). Preservation of a series of historically significant Victorian warehouse buildings in downtown Cleveland that has created a new mixed-use residential neighborhood in the heart of Cleveland.

CONTACT

Parkside Preservation
James Brown, Executive Director
P.O. Box 15527
Philadelphia, PA 19131
Telephone: 215-473-4900
Fax: 215-477-7734

RUDY BRUNER AWARD FOR URBAN EXCELLENCE

BRUNER FOUNDATION
130 Prospect Street
Cambridge, MA 02139
PH: 617.492.8404
FX: 617.876.4002

www.brunerfoundation.org

RUDY BRUNER AWARD FOR URBAN EXCELLENCE

LEARNING ABOUT URBAN EXCELLENCE

INTRODUCTION

Each cycle of the Rudy Bruner Award forges an understanding of urban excellence by asking a distinguished Committee of urban experts to examine, evaluate, and interpret the values embodied in five places. Committee members are not simply jurists; they are also students, learning from each other and from the winners. Their discussions are challenging and risky, demanding self-examination as well as judgment. People who are used to "knowing" are asked to make their perspectives vulnerable to expertise outside their disciplines. This vulnerability creates a climate of listening and a patient search for a deeper understanding of urban excellence. Thus what may begin as a series of assertions around the Selection Committee table becomes the construction of a shared set of values, among candidate submissions and among Selection Committee members, which can then be employed in identifying the Gold Medal winner.

This year's deliberations returned again and again to the concept of commitment to place and placemaking. Learning from the five projects, the Selection Committee sounded an unusually clear call for an urban excellence that engendered not only commitment to place, but also to the processes involved in making and sustaining places. This expanded concept of place, collaboratively developed during the course of the Selection Committee work, stands as an interdisciplinary common ground. Economic, social, political, design, and managerial insight all led the Committee to conclude that commitment to place in this year's program was embodied in processes that were iterative, inclusive, conducive to learning, able to build capacity and consensus in the community, conflict resolving, evolving, oriented to grassroots constituencies, contextual, and focused on both project design and economics. If this list seems dauntingly exhaustive, consider the Committee's suggestion that all of these elements of good process belong to a single overarching approach: commitment to place expressed through a commitment to "placemaking." Placemaking occurs when local communities work together to create, recreate, and care for urban places, and in so doing strengthen and empower themselves. This work, literally taking place on common ground, can only be sustained by the kind of hardheaded democratic processes recognized by the Selection Committee. And, importantly, such work must be sustained: the process of placemaking does not end when a place has been built; it is an ongoing activity that maintains, sustains, and renews places and communities as they evolve over time.

THE EVOLUTION OF PLACE

The 1999 Selection Committee placed a particular value on the responsiveness of the product to community processes and to changing circumstances. Yerba Buena Gardens, for example, started as a grand but exclusive vision of a financial district "fortress" safely protected by skyscrapers from what was described by some as surrounding blight. As the strategies for implementing the vision began to incorporate more constituencies and agendas, the ultimate goal itself began to change, transforming to reflect the needs and aspirations of those involved in defining and creating the place. Some of the original vision survives to this day, but it has been enriched by different perspectives and an expanded set of possibilities. Evolution cast aside some traits — office buildings, for example — while adding others: affordable housing, Zeum, the bowling alley, and a variety of community programs. Ultimately, the project became a mixed-use development around a large public garden that contributes significantly to both the city of San Francisco and the immediate South of Market neighborhood.

Like Yerba Buena, the National AIDS Memorial Grove began with a strong vision, in this case for a "living memorial" devoted to those affected by the AIDS epidemic. Also like Yerba Buena, this core vision proved inspiring enough to sustain the project while remaining sufficiently flexible to adapt to change. The actual design, for example, evolved from the initial conception of a ginkgo grove to the final plan for a landscaped dell. The expansion of naming opportunities was another departure from the original concept, this one driven by financial need. Most important, however, was the evolution of the volunteer workdays. Originally seen as a strategy to get the memorial built, these workdays became central to the meaning and purposes of the place. In a very real way, they became part of the memorial itself. As much as the different physical dimensions of the Grove, these workdays shape how people interact with and use the space, and have created a level of commitment that reaches deep into the community.

The Grove's workdays also provide an example of how placemaking continues long after a place has been "finished." The memorial continues to change as new constituencies participate in its development and maintenance, and as the AIDS epidemic itself changes over time. This kind of ongoing placemaking can also be seen in the collaborative structures that oversee the maintenance, operations, and future development at Yerba Buena — structures that, not accidentally, resemble the democratic processes out of which the project was ultimately forged. Such efforts to ensure continued collaborative oversight also appear in the Portland Public Market, where wage structures and the point-of-sale system permit constant dialogue in a context of mutual commitment. In Parkside Preservation, such structures are still incipient, since the communities living in the neighborhood are less prepared than other winners to organize and fully represent themselves in the development process. However, the collaboration of social service providers and faith-based organizations with businesses, outside investors, and James Brown's own organization gives a strong foreshadowing of what might evolve. And while ARTScorpsLA is by far the least structured of this year's winners, the radically evolving usage of the artparks reveals a commitment to continued democratic involvement.

ARTScorpsLA also illustrates another, subtler aspect of the idea of the evolution of place: the acceptance of fragility and impermanence in the urban landscape. No place lasts forever. But the art of placemaking suggests that perhaps no place is ever "completed" at all. If taken to its logical extreme — as it was by Tricia Ward at ARTScorpsLA — this reasoning leads to a kind of planning that not only takes into account but actually relies upon constant change. In the artparks, the narrative of creation loses its "climax" — completion — and becomes a continuous and ongoing story of construction and maintenance. ARTScorpsLA's artparks were built during a discrete period of time, but the actual construction was only one manifestation of the relationships and community activities that sat at the heart of the project. The parks therefore remain open to different users and attendant changes, like the entrance and departure of the "Old Gangsters" and the basketball courts. Since la Culebra was never "completed," there have been fewer barriers to reprogramming it to suit the wishes of the communities that use and maintain it.

In sum, the values embodied in the places were seen by the Selection Committee as the basis for their ongoing care. The making of place and the ongoing care of place belonged to the same evolutionary ideal — a process that continually enriches places and their underlying visions, animates action based on shared need, remains inclusive, improves relationships among participants, and engenders long-term caring for place.

INCLUSIVE PLACEMAKING

Crucial to the kind of responsive evolution envisioned by the Selection Committee is a commitment to inclusiveness in both place and process. At its most basic level, this means that the evolutionary schema outlined above must be grounded in an essentially democratic dialogue among the various communities associated with a place. This space for discussion must be carefully constructed so that powerful players and experts are made vulnerable to the "view from below" provided by community groups, local residents, social service providers, and other stakeholders. This is not intended to undermine the experts, but to ensure that their expertise is used in the most beneficial and context-appropriate ways, rather than simply exerting itself according to its own momentum and logic. Again Yerba Buena provides an excellent example of this: the lawsuits created a space in which major players like the Redevelopment Agency were forced to discuss the project with area residents who felt marginalized by the process. Design, financial, and development expertise produced little until local residents and youth were fully vested in the process.

The fact that Yerba Buena's inclusiveness came about as the result of such bitter disagreements illustrates the fact that a good process often emerges from the dynamics of conflict. An inclusive process can, in fact, often be the most expedient, most efficient, and ultimately most successful model of development available - despite its arduousness, inefficiency, and daunting challenges. One is reminded of the saying about democracy: it is the worst system, except for any other. If the dialogue between stakeholders is not sturdy, practical, and realistic, it may not be able to contain all the conflict that inevitably attends any serious urban intervention. Indeed, many of this year's projects suggest that such dialogues must be institutionalized, in the kinds of structures for ongoing placemaking described earlier.

Inclusive processes, the Selection Committee found, seem to produce inclusive places. Parkside Preservation resulted in well-restored mansions — immediately rented to special needs populations.

ARTScorpsLA transformed urban dumpsites into unique community artparks — which were then open to all locals, including gang members. Portland Public Market created a powerful shopper and tourist magnet — which also housed an innovative restaurant run by the clients of a nearby social service provider. The workdays at the AIDS Memorial Grove are open to anyone, allowing participation of the full diversity of people affected by the epidemic. Yerba Buena, of course, has integrated this inclusiveness in countless ways, from the programming of the arts facilities and the garden to the Tai Chi park and low-income housing. In each case a place that might have been committed only to wooing tourist dollars, or at least to serving the needs of a narrow portion of the local community, instead became an authentic part of its urban habitat.

The Selection Committee was also impressed with the fact that many of this year's finalists included young people — an unusual attitude in contemporary urban projects. In some places, like Yerba Buena, this willingness was hard-won, as the area's young people organized and advocated for elements that they deemed important. Yerba Buena ultimately met the youths more than halfway with Zeum, the day care center, the arts opportunities, and the other youth facilities. ARTScorpsLA depended on young people from the beginning, mobilizing youthful energy to build and fill the artparks. The various artistic opportunities provided through the program reinforce ARTScorpsLA's commitment to inner city youth.

Other projects have incorporated young people as well. The AIDS Grove, for example, has evolved into a place where students of all ages come to volunteer and learn about the epidemic and about gay and lesbian issues. The "food theater" at Portland Public Market not only draws in adult shoppers, but begins to build an understanding of local food production in ways that can capture the imagination of children. These kinds of practices, the Selection Committee felt, were very impressive at a time when youths are often "designed out" of urban places because they are seen as a destabilizing enemy to a safe urban environment. The inclusion of the young reflects faith in the placemaking process: by bringing them into the process in meaningful ways, these places have persuaded young people to invest themselves in their communities, incorporating them as sources of positive energy and activity. As one Selection Committee member explained,

> *As a society, we don't honor our youth enough. The issue for our generation is to deal with the generation gap by empowering our youth more than we have in the past. We should be tool makers for young people to help them grow past the culture of immediate gratification.*

COMMITMENT TO PLACE

One undeniable fact stands out in these descriptions of inclusive evolutionary processes of placemaking: they require a lot of work. None of the themes identified by the Selection Committee are easy to achieve, and though they might ultimately be the least problematic way to proceed, they promise challenging work with uncertain rewards. What, then, motivates people to begin and to sustain such processes? The answer, the Committee came to believe, is best described as commitment to place. By this, the Committee meant the kind of commitment epitomized by James Brown in Parkside: to the place for what it could be, but also for its history, what is currently there, and who is currently there. The envisioned future, in other words, builds on and affirms the existing place and the human communities and relationships attached to it. This kind of commitment is powerful enough to draw other stakeholders into the project, enabling quality placemaking to proceed. Yerba Buena balanced the profit potential of its choice location with homes and programming for local residents; Parkside took advantage of historic mansions to help fund special needs housing for locals; ARTScorpsLA turned unpleasant and unused urban dumps into artparks for local communities; and the Portland Public Market marshaled local materials and contractors to construct a strategic urban intervention designed to complement already existing patterns of central city use.

The kind of commitment to place embodied in these projects does more than make collaborative efforts possible; it also serves as the basis for community building. The Selection Committee noted that caring for places can provide a common ground that actually fosters relationships between people and communities, making it easier to build the kind of institutionalized dialogues that lie at the heart of placemaking. Thus the process of creating Yerba Buena had the effect of producing not only buildings, but organizations like TODCO, the Yerba Buena Alliance, and the places-with-faces maintenance group that sustain both the body and spirit of the project. The National AIDS Memorial Grove provides a focus for gay and lesbian groups and AIDS activism, and the workdays in particular serve to strengthen bonds between participants from diverse segments of the community. Parkside Preservation and ARTScorpsLA are still some distance from producing mature community organizations, but they have already engendered a level of activism and community self-awareness that may well have been unthinkable before the projects began. At a more generalized level, the Portland Public Market's mission includes educating Maine's shoppers about their citizenship in a statewide agricultural economy, raising their awareness of where their dollars go and persuading them to participate more actively in keeping the state's family farms viable.

Another byproduct of the commitment to place is the aspiration to create the very best place possible. Each of these projects came about in response to needs and goals that could easily have been met at a more minimal level. Certainly many blighted neighborhoods have been renewed without the elaborate restorations completed in Parkside, or the world-famous architecture that graces Yerba Buena. A community-built and community-maintained local park does not necessarily conjure up images of meaningful artistic visions like those created by ARTScorpsLA. The Portland Public Market and the AIDS Grove, too, were conceived as well-designed and beautiful places that make significant aesthetic contributions to the urban fabric. The Selection Committee felt that such high aspirations eventually mattered on more levels than the aesthetic. In Parkside, for example, the restorations allowed special needs populations to be housed without triggering present or future "not-in-my-back-yard" syndromes. In all the projects, the commitment to include locals was dignified by the quality of design in the places created — places that testify to the pride in the places local constituencies have created together.

Quality design and community pride stand out all the more starkly for the desperate situations in which these urban interventions were born: neighborhoods ruined by slash-and-burn urban renewal, financial crises, riots, or slow urban decay; populations decimated by an epidemic, poverty, social ills of every kind; buildings vacant or destroyed. This kind of hardship, ultimately, can sometimes provide the galvanizing force required to begin pioneering work in urban placemaking. Not all placemaking need be heroic, but this year's finalists all represent significant successes in the least hospitable of locales. The Bruner site visit teams always interviewed at least one person who shook their heads and said, "no one in their right minds would have thought of doing *that*," whether *that* was putting the San Francisco MoMA South of Market, restoring a burnt-out beer master's mansion in Parkside, clearing the used needles and other garbage from the de Laveaga Dell, investing in a new public market in depressed downtown Portland, or marshaling Latino youths to retake urban dumpsites from reluctant absentee landlords. All of these projects, the Selection Committee noted, turned entrenched urban problems into opportunities. In the chaotic quilt of hard times, new relationships can be forged and new possibilities imagined and realized, especially if placemakers are willing to make their vision a shared one and open themselves to the contributions of others.

A PRACTICAL IDEALISM

Despite the idealism inherent in the Selection Committee's concept of urban excellence, Committee members felt that excellence firmly belongs in the "real" world of practicality as much as in the idealistic world of inclusiveness and democratic dialogues. The Committee took care to recognize that old-fashioned economic savvy and creative financing are by no means antithetical to the collaborative evolutionary processes that they discerned in this year's finalists. Several projects faced considerable economic challenges, and full awareness of and respect for these challenges was a critical factor in their success. Yerba Buena, for example, shrewdly traded against its commercial profit potential to make possible its social justice and cultural agendas, while in Parkside the historic preservation and low income tax credits allowed neighborhood renewal to proceed. The National AIDS Memorial Grove acknowledged fiscal realities by promising to fund the gardener in perpetuity and by providing more naming opportunities to achieve that goal. The Portland Public Market faced very few economic constraints, but its developers are fully aware that unless individual vendors can turn a profit, the market is at risk; thus they have allowed for constant fine tuning through the point-of-sale system. Finally, ARTScorpsLA's guerrilla strategies — just take the land if it is not being used — grew out of the scarcity of community resources.

Economics are not the only place where practical creativity and common sense were of value in this year's finalists. Collaborative processes do not obviate the need for problem solving and hard critical work; they only create a context where solutions can be found and implemented successfully. The idea of putting the Convention Center underground at Yerba Buena, for example, made the gardens and many of the other facilities possible. The inspiration to house special needs populations in the refurbished mansions of Parkside neatly managed the difficult feat of balancing local needs with development goals. The decision to embrace and expand the volunteer workdays at the National AIDS Memorial Grove not only made the project possible, but extended its reach beyond the de Laveaga Dell and into the lives of those who participated. In these cases and many others, placemakers continued to produce "urban pioneer" style ideas even as they worked within a context of collaboration and democratic purpose. This suggests that pioneering urban innovations need not emanate from a top-down traditional leadership style, but can also emerge from a more grassroots placemaking effort.

This mentality does not mean that the Committee declared inspired or visionary leadership to be unimportant. It remains critical. Again, the best example of this comes from Parkside, where James Brown's energy and commitment has been almost solely responsible for powering the project through the decades. His leadership, however, has been intimately intertwined with a commitment to the neighborhood and the people of Parkside, with the ultimate goal of helping create a genuine neighborhood where such singular leadership could give way to more broad-based community coalitions. Brown's instinct for inclusiveness appears in his cooperation with the outside investors PHPC, and in his ties with local service providers and organizations. This sort of visionary leadership tied to collaborative goals can also be seen in Helen Sause of the San Francisco Redevelopment Authority; her willingness to share responsibility for the project only enriched her commitment to the inspirational, world-class vision of Yerba Buena Gardens. And few projects have witnessed the kind of collaborate-at-all-costs attitude of Tricia Ward at ARTScorpsLA. In each case, the advantages of strong leadership based on visionary ideas and inspirational energy were retained even in a process that embraced inefficient, conflict-ridden, and (in a word) democratic progress.

PLACES FOR PEOPLE, PEOPLE FOR PLACES

In the final analysis, the placemaking concepts that emerged from the Selection Committee deliberations stress the importance of relationships among people as well as the relationships between people and place. The complex processes involved in the evolution of urban places are, in that sense, quite simple: they are the kinds of processes that result from merging the social logic of democracy with the architectural logic of physical planning and urban design. Such an approach is pragmatic in the best American tradition, valuing what is useful and beneficial to those who will use and benefit from it. It is also democratic, ensuring that those people using and benefiting from a place are the people who have a stake in it — its citizens, so to speak.

To a certain extent, this notion of urban excellence can be seen as a corrective to urban planning visions that over-emphasize the technical expertise of planners and architects, seeking instead to draw professional expertise into a context where it will most benefit the people and communities attached to an urban place. The result, as this year's winners illustrate, are technically good and beautiful places that support diverse communities and encourage community members to become stakeholders in their neighborhoods.

One clue that this delicate balance between technical and social excellence has been successfully struck can be seen in the fact that Yerba Buena, the Portland Public Market, the National AIDS Memorial Grove, ARTScorpsLA, and Parkside Preservation all celebrate the ordinary experiences of everyday life, be it: people doing Tai Chi in the park; shopping in the Portland Market; working through the pain involved when one's life has is touched by the AIDS epidemic; struggling to raise children in poor communities in Los Angeles or Philadelphia; sustaining family farms in Maine; or simply pausing for coffee or a cup of "stone" soup on a busy day.

To be sure, this year's winners also represent the celebration of the extraordinary as well: Botta's San Francisco MoMA, and the Yerba Buena Center for the Arts by Polshek and Maki; the discovery and representation of cultural myths within former garbage dumps in the barrios of Los Angeles; the celebration of food origins and sources as part of consumer education in Maine; the substantial restoration of parkside mansions in Philadelphia; and a former needle park reborn as a national memorial to all those touched by the AIDS epidemic.

How were these extraordinary mixtures of the everyday and the transcendent created? The investigations and discussions that led to the 1999 Rudy Bruner Awards revealed that these successes were not accidental, nor were they unique to their locations. Rather, they came out of patient, arduous, everyday decisions to commit to a place and its peoples; out of an ability to recognize problems to be solved while remaining open to new ways of solving them; and out of a willingness to include all players in both process and project. The coming together of these relatively simple elements grows out of the courage to challenge conventional wisdom, and out of faith in the importance of place and the possibilities of placemaking.

The projects awarded the Gold and Silver Rudy Bruner Award Medals in 1999 are intentionally vulnerable and risky in a climate where one might expect to see pressure for increased power and a reduction of risk. They are each in their own way incomplete, in a world that values comprehensive and complete solutions to the challenges of the day. And they are inefficient and in some ways uncertain in cultures that seem to value efficiency and an economy of means above all else. The courage and democratic faith embodied in such decisions, and the resulting quality places they produced, can be an inspiration to us as we seek to make excellent urban places.

BIBLIOGRAPHY

BRUNER BOOKS

Philip Langdon with Robert Shibley and Polly Welch, *Urban Excellence* (New York: Van Nostrand Reinhold, 1990).

Neal Peirce and Robert Guskind, *Breakthroughs: Re-creating the American City* (New Brunswick, NJ: Center for Urban Policy Research, Rutgers, State University of NJ, 1993).

Jay Farbstein and Richard Wener, *1991 Rudy Bruner Award for Excellence in the Urban Environment: Connections: Creating Urban Excellence* (Boston: Bruner Foundation, Inc., 1992).

Jay Farbstein and Richard Wener, *1993 Rudy Bruner Award for Excellence in the Urban Environment: Rebuilding Communities: Re-creating Urban Excellence* (Boston: Bruner Foundation, Inc., 1993).

Jay Farbstein and Richard Wener, *1995 Rudy Bruner Award for Excellence in the Urban Environment: Building Coalitions for Urban Excellence,* (Boston: Bruner Foundation, Inc., 1996).

Jay Farbstein and Richard Wener, *1997 Rudy Bruner Award for Excellence in the Urban Environment: Visions of Urban Excellence* (Boston: Bruner Foundation, Inc., 1998).

Jay Farbstein, Robert Shibley, Polly Welch, and Richard Wener, with Axelrod, *Sustaining Urban Excellence: Learning from the Rudy Bruner Award for Urban Excellence 1987-1993* (Boston: Bruner Foundation, Inc., 1998).

YERBA BUENA GARDENS

Anon., "Entertainment and Retail Center, San Francisco, California, Simon Martin-Vegue Winkelstein Moris and Gary E. Handel Associates," *Architecture,* (vol.84, Jan. 1995, n.1, p.38-39).

Anon., "The thirteen attractions of Yerba Buena." *Art Newspaper* (v. 6, Jan. 1995, p. 9).

Anon., "James Stewart Polshek: Center for the Arts Theater at Yerba Buena Gardens, San Francisco, CA 1985-1993." *A + U: architecture and urbanism* (vol. 11(302), Nov. 1995, p.34-45).

Anon., "Maki in San Francisco = In the centre of downtown." Arca (vol.98, Nov. 1995, p.54-59).

Auchmutey, Pam, "South of Market gets new lease on life." *Buildings Design Journal* (vol. 3(10), Oct. 1985, p.8.)

Baker, Kenneth. "Rising spirits (Bay Area art scene)." *Art News* (v. 93, May 1994, p. 128-9).

Bisel, Clark, "Place making at Yerba Buena Gardens," *Urban Land* (1994 Mar., v.53, n.3, p.8-9).

Betsky, Aaron. "Yerba Buena Gardens: buildings in search of a plan." *Architectural Record.* (v. 180, Apr. 1992, p. 29).

Bloomfield, Anne, "A history of the California historical society's new mission street neighborhood," in *California History* (Winter 1995/6, p. 372).

Canty, Donald. "Combining artistry and compassion (public housing remodeled for senior citizens in San Francisco, Yerba Buena Plaza Annex)." *Architecture.* (v. 74, July 1985, p. 49-53).

Clifton, Leigh Ann. "Decision in San Francisco (the future of the Yerba Buena Gardens Cultural Center remains uncertain)." *Artweek* (v. 22, Feb. 7 1991, p. 13).

Clifton, Leigh Ann. "New problems for veteran nonprofit arts venues (in San Francisco)." *Artweek.* (v. 25, Apr. 7 1994, p. 13).

Elberling, John, "An urban layer cake," *SF Bay Guardian* 11/17/93, 14-15.

Hartmann, Chester and Alvin Averoach, et al., *Yerba Buena: Land Grab and Community Resistance in San Francisco* (San Francisco: Glide Publications, 1974).

Ho, Cathy Lang. "San Francisco shake-up." *Architecture* (v. 87, Feb. 1998, p. 40-41).

Jenkins, Steven. "Old and in the way: Stories of the city (Yerba Buena Gardens Cultural Center, San Francisco)." *Artweek* (v. 22, June 6 1991, p. 13-14).

Jewell, Linda. "When green isn't good enough (Esplanade at Yerba Buena Gardens, San Francisco, Calif). *Landscape Architecture.* (v. 84, Aug. 1994, p. 36-7).

Kaufman, Jason Edward. "Skid-row revived by culture and commerce (South of Market neighborhood)." *Art Newspaper* (v. 6, Jan. 1995, p. 8).

Kaufman, Jason Edward. "Multiculturalism without political correctness (something for everyone at the Yerba Center)." *Art Newspaper* (v. 6, Jan. 1995, p. 9).

Krainak, Paul. "The heart of San Francisco." *New Art Examiner* (v. 22, Summer 1995, p. 31).

Moffat, David. "Yerba Buena schemes unveiled in San Francisco." *Architecture* (v. 81, Apr. 1992, p. 23).

Myers, Martin, "Yerba Buena Gardens, San Francisco." *The Canadian Architect.* (v. 32, Oct. 1987, p. 41).

Parker, Cheryl, "Making a 21st century neighborhood." (Masters Thesis, UC Berkely, 1993). Partially reprinted as "Making a 21st century neighborhood," in *Places* (vol 10 #1, 1995, pp. 36-45).

Parker, Cheryl, "A story of change: re-making SF."

Pearson, Clifford A., "Metreon, San Francisco, California: What's a shopping and entertainment center doing in an arts complex? Keeping the place busy around the clock," *Architectural Record* (Volume 10, 1999).

Pollock, Naomi, "Silver palette: Center for the Arts, Yerba Buena Gardens Galleries and Forum, San Francisco, California." *Architectural Record* (1994 Mar., v.182, n.3, p.[72]-79).

Smith, Irvin. "The Human mark: Yerba Buena Gardens Center, San Francisco." *Artweek* (v. 22, Apr. 11 1991, p. 13-14).

Sullivan, Ann C. "Entertainment and retail center, San Francisco." *Architecture* (v. 84, Jan. 1995, p. 38-9).

Wagner, Michael. "Artistic efforts (three new projects for Yerba Buena Center)." *Interiors* (New York, N.Y.) (v. 148, May 1989, p. 314).

Wetmore, Robert and Sause, Helen, "Striking a public/private deal." *Urban Land* (1995 Jan., v.54, n.1, p. 25-28).

Wetmore, Robert, and Sause, Helen, "Sony entertainment center breaks ground." *Urban Land* (1997 Aug., v.56, n.8, p. 24-25).

Woodbridge, Sally Byrne. "Topping off Yerba Buena (Gardens, San Francisco)." *Progressive Architecture.* (v. 67, Mar. 1986, p. 22-3).

Woodbridge, Sally, "SF tries again with Yerba Buena." *Progressive architecture* (1989 Oct., v.70, no.10, p. 27-28).

Woodbridge, Sally B., "When good urban plans go awry (Yerba Buena Gardens, San Francisco)." *Progressive Architecture* (v. 76, Nov. 1995, p. 60-7).

http://yerbabuena.org

PORTLAND PUBLIC MARKET

Anon., "Design awards [New Jersey Society of Architects 1991 Design Awards Competition, includes Hugh Boyd of Portland Public Market]." *Architecture New Jersey* (1992, v.28, no.1, p. 9-24).

Fox, Nancy, "Case study: Pike Place Market, Seattle," in Bernard J. Frieden and Lynne B. Sagalyn, eds., *Downtown, Inc.: How America Rebuilds Cities* (Cambridge, MA: MIT Press, 1989).

Merrill, Meadow Rue, "Portland project will give farm goods a gourmet touch," *Boston Sunday Globe,* August 16, 1998, pp. B10, B12.

Spitzer, Theodore and Hilary Baum, *Public Markets and Community Revitalization* (Urban Land Institute and Project for Public Spaces, Inc., 1995).

http://www.portlandmarket.com/main/didyouknow.html

NATIONAL AIDS MEMORIAL GROVE

Hart, Jane Turner, *Innovations in park and open space stewardship: Case studies and examples in urban park and open space management,* (San Francisco: The Trust for Public Land, 1996).

Heyman, Harriet, "A healing landscape: SF designers honor people with AIDS," *Garden Design* (August / September 1998).

Stevens, M. "Golden Gate Grove. . . Project for an AIDS memorial grove in Golden Gate Park's De-Laveaga Dell." *Landscape Architecture* (84: (8) 22-& AUG 1994).

http://www.aidsmemorial.org

ARTSCORPSLA

Dickerson, Amina and Tricia Ward, "A co-meditation on youth, art, and society," in Mary Jane Jacob and Michael Brenson, eds., *Conversations at the Castle* (The MIT PRESS, 1998), pp. 150-60.

Dunitz, Robin J. and James Prigoff, *Painting the Town, Murals of California,* (R.J.D. Enterprises, 1997). See also pp. 200 "Earth Memories" on an ARTScorpLA mural.

Jacob, Mary Jane, and Michael Brenson and Eva M. Olson, *Culture in Action: A Public Art Program of Sculpture Chicago,* (Bay Press, Inc. 1995).

PARKSIDE PRESERVATION

Jenkins, Mark, "His lifetime goal: saving neighborhood (Parkside, Philadelphia)." *Historic Preservation.* (v. 37, June 1985, p. 30).

Jenkins, Mark, "How entrepreneurs do it." *Historic Preservation* (1985 June, v.37, no.3, p.[28-33]).

Lee, Antoinette, "Livable communities." *CRM:* [bulletin] (1994, v.17, n.2, p. 26-27).

Miller, Zane, and Bruce Tucker, *Changing Plans for America's Inner Cities: Cincinnati's Over-the-Rhine and Twentieth-Century Urbanism (*Columbus: Ohio State University Press, 1998).

Morse, Susan, "Mansions reborn: a Trust-aided rehab produces much-needed low-income housing in Philadelphia," *Historic Preservation* 1989 Sept.-Oct., v.41, no.5, p. 59-62.

Sweeney, Thomas, "Steady progress revitalizes Parkside: distressed Philadelphia neighborhood finds a champion. *Historic Preservation News* (1993 June, v.33, n.5, p. 20-21).

FOR FURTHER READING ABOUT PLACEMAKING

Casey, Edward S. *Getting Back Into Place: Toward a Renewed Understanding of the Place-World* (Bloomington, IN: Indiana University Press, 1993).

Hiss, T. *The Experience of Place* (New York: Random House, 1991)

Schneekloth, Lynda and Shibley, Robert. *Placemaking: The Art and Practice of Building Communities* (New York: John Wiley & Sons, Inc., 1995).

Tuan Yi-Fu. *Space and Place: The Perspective of Experience* (Minneapolis: University of Minnesota Press, 1977).